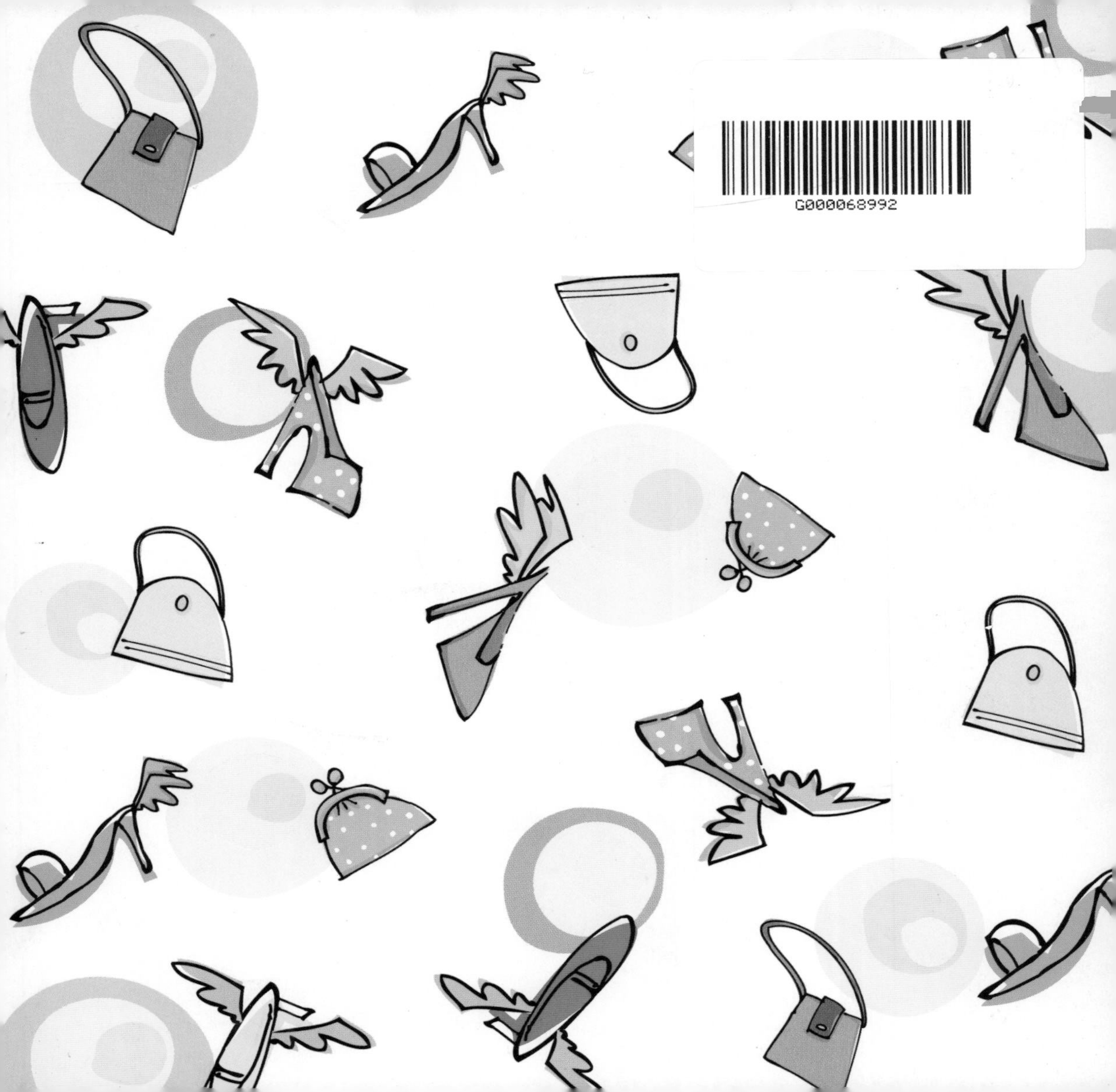

B²

Born to Shop®

Born to Shop®

Modern Woman . . . Worship her like the Goddess she is

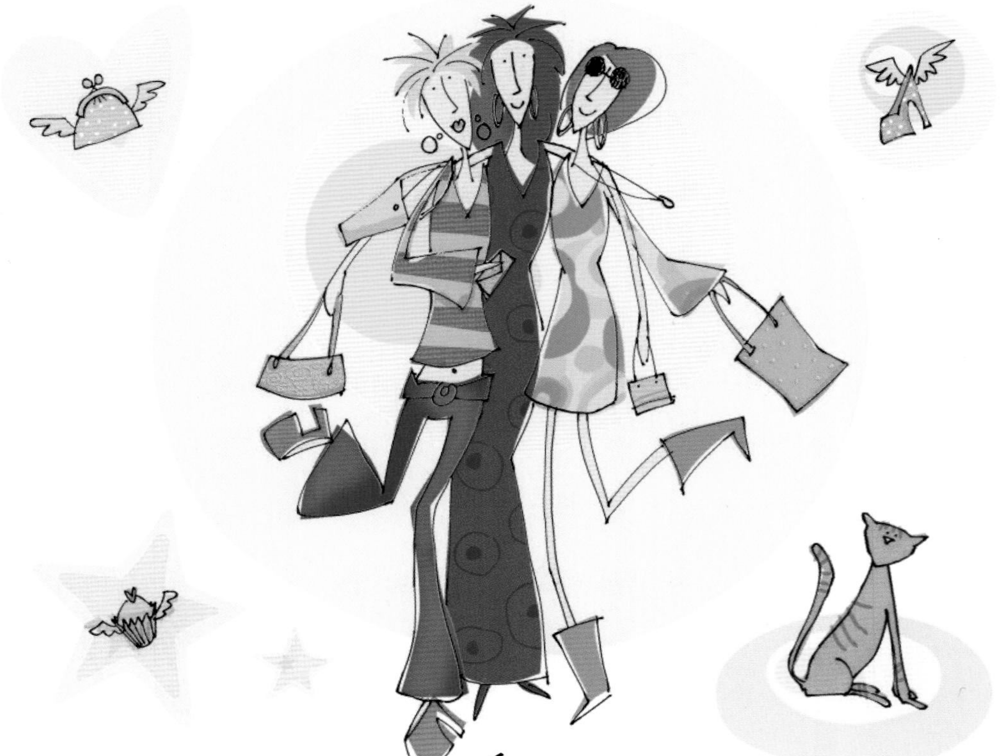

PRION

This is a Prion book

First published in Great Britain in 2010 by Prion
An imprint of the Carlton Publishing Group
20 Mortimer Street
London W1T 3JW

ISBN: 978-1-85375-773-0

Printed in Dubai

Contents

Born to be Beautiful

I know I'm not perfect, but I'm so close it scares me

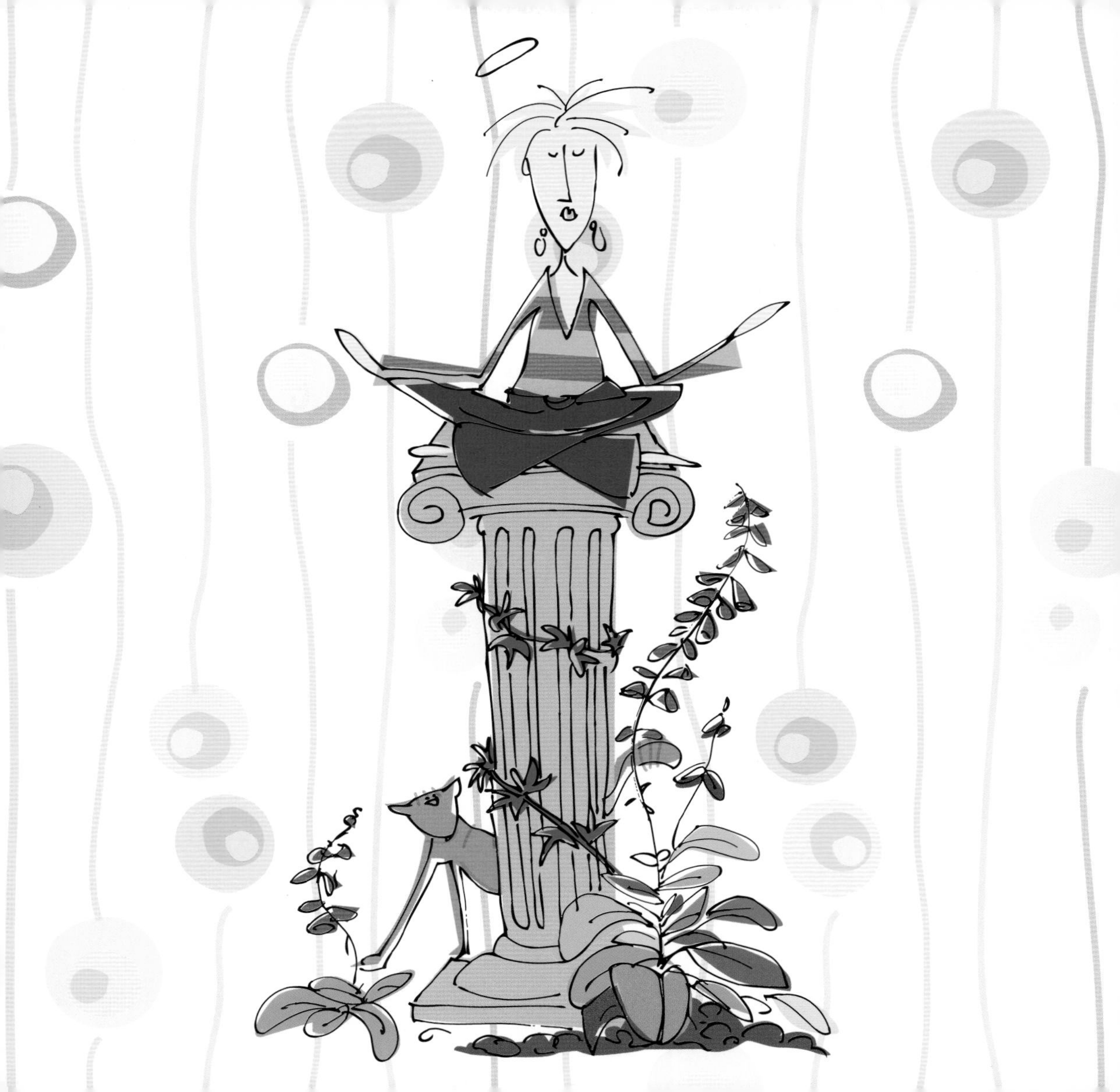

I may be late but I'm worth the wait

10

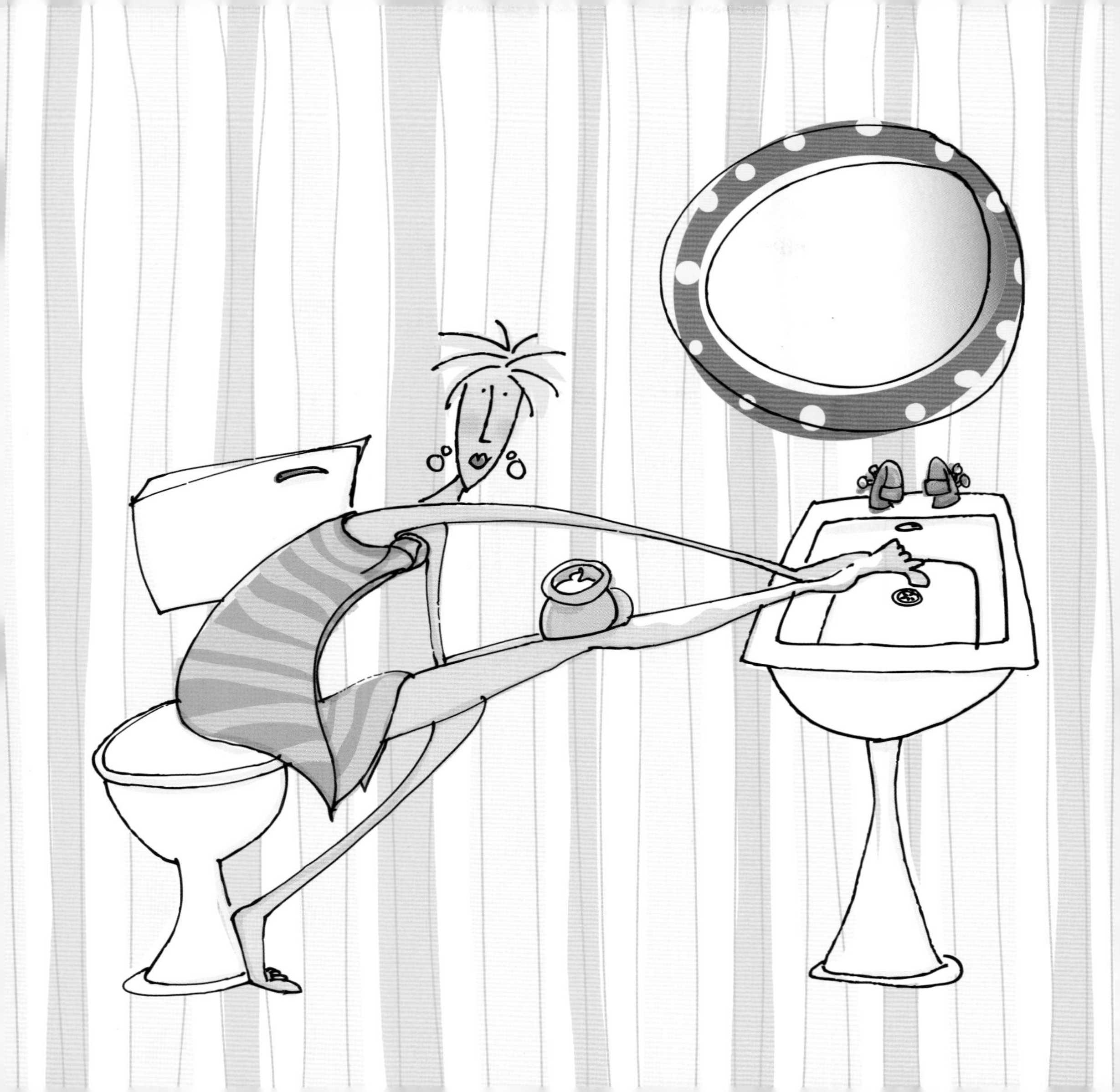

High maintenance...
but worth it

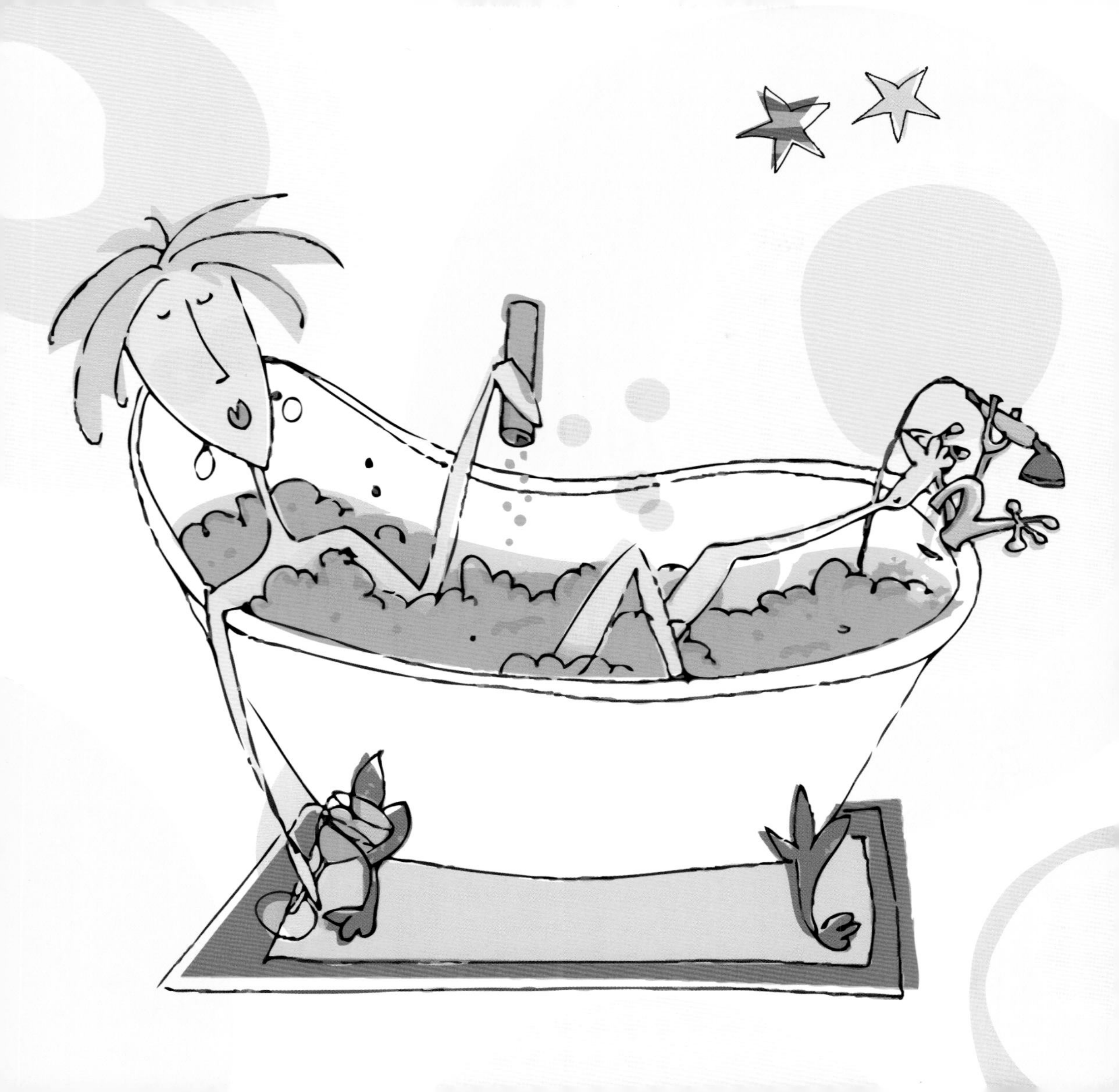

I'm usually gorgeous
but it's my day off

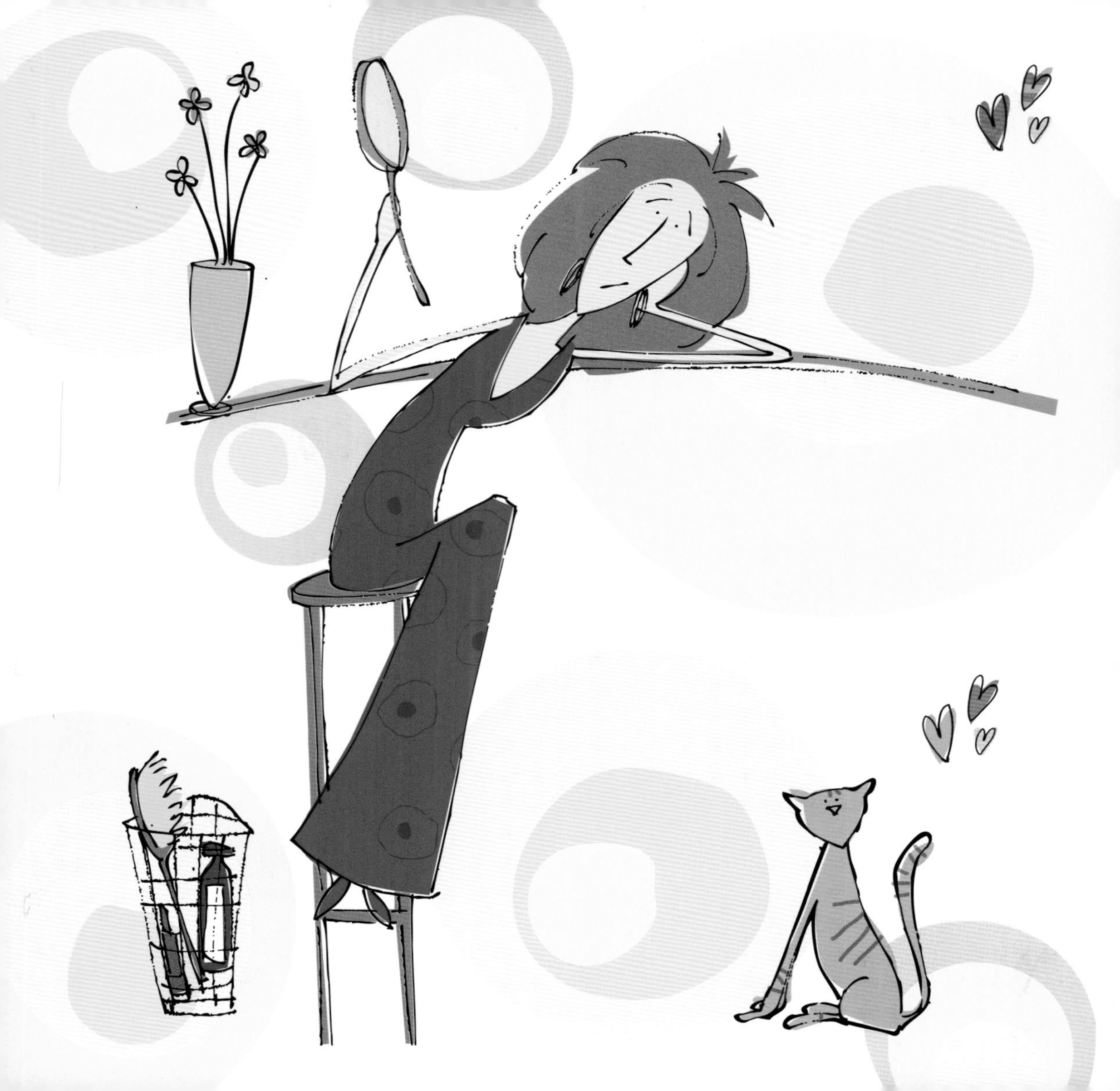

Too much of a good
thing is wonderful

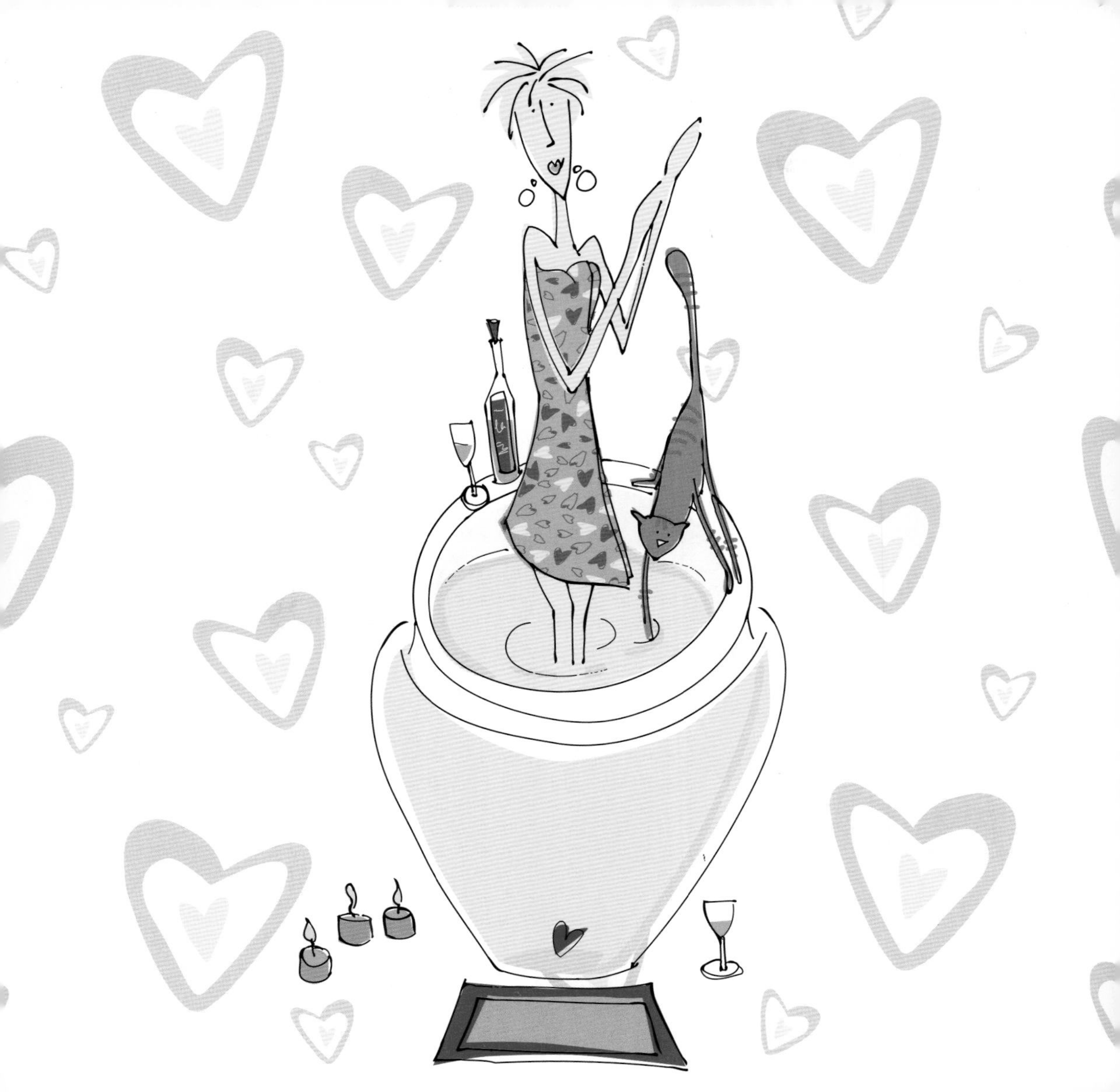

It's all
about
me

I didn't ask to be a Princess...

...but if the crown fits!

Worship me like
the Goddess I am

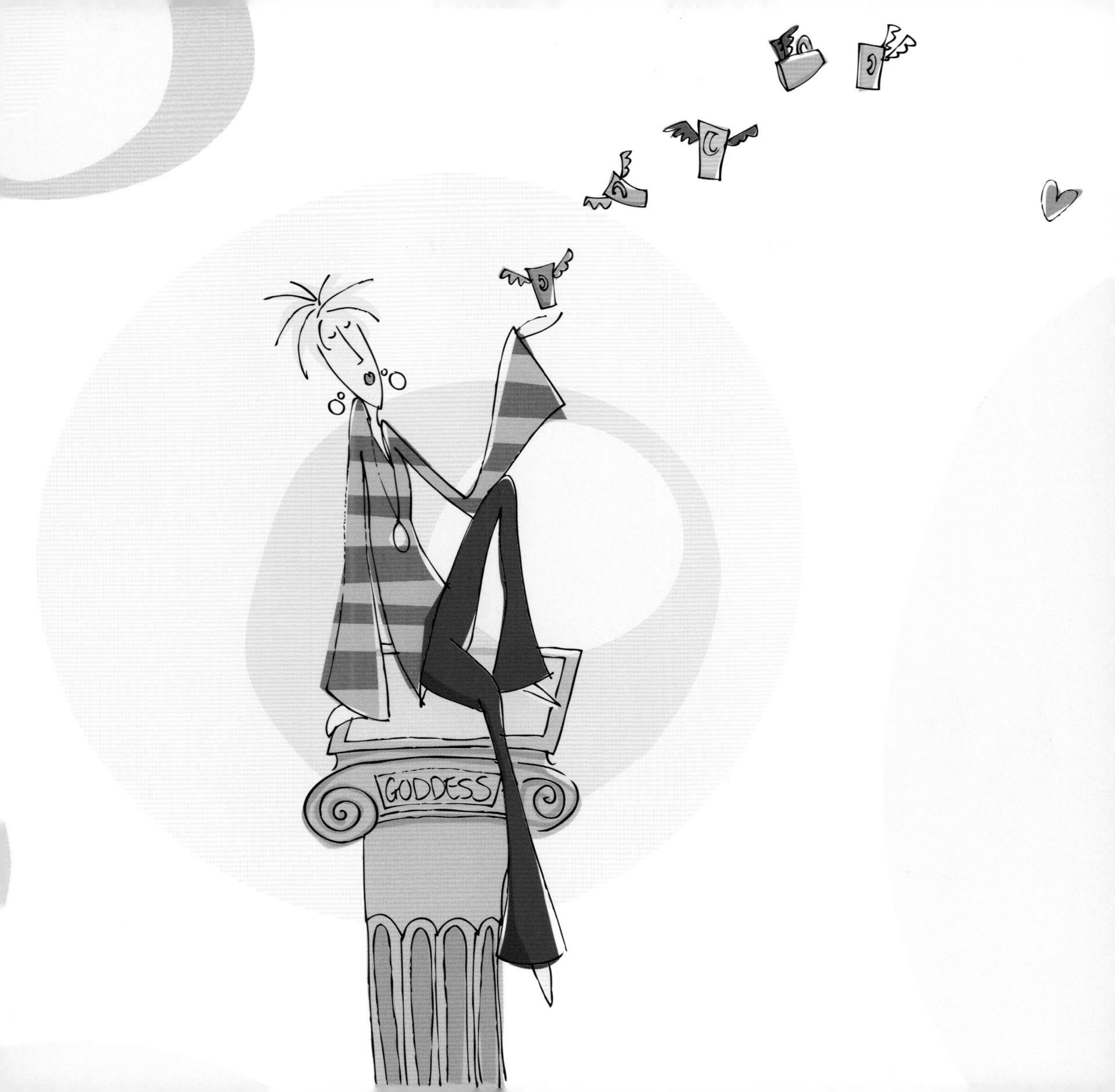
GODDESS

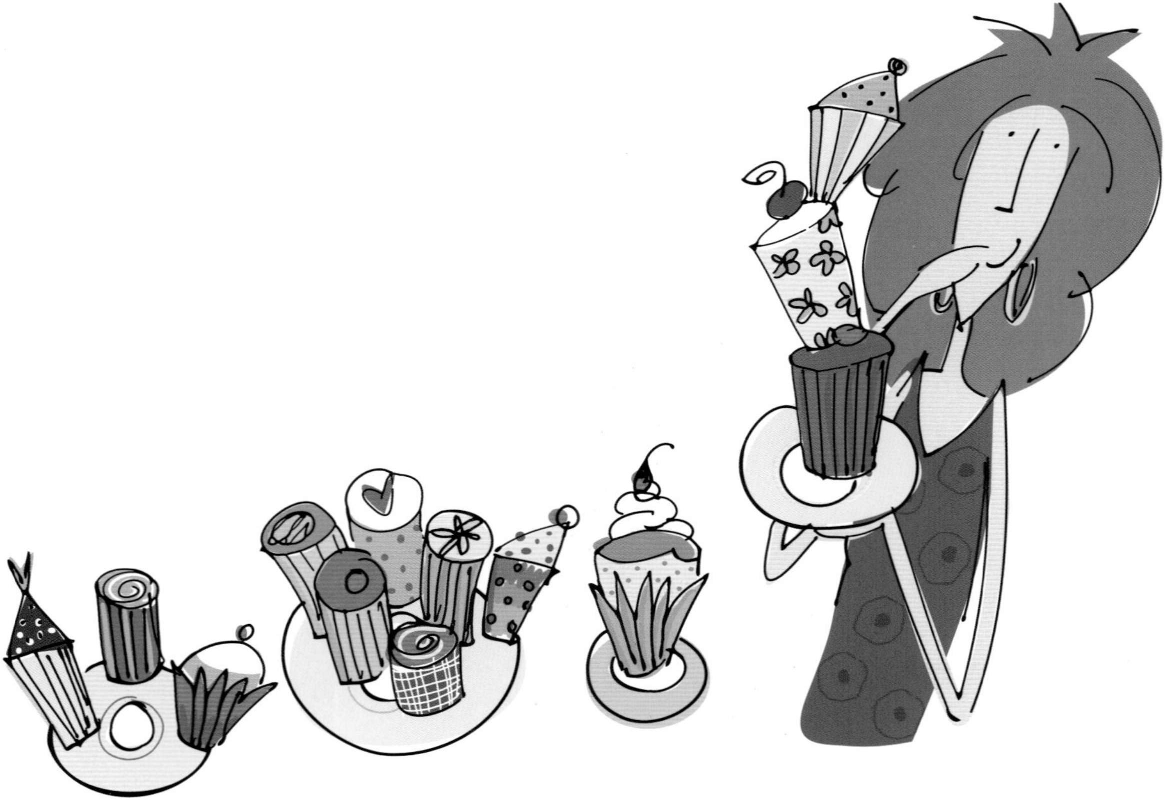

Born to Eat,
Forced to Diet

I'd give up chocolate
but I'm no quitter

24

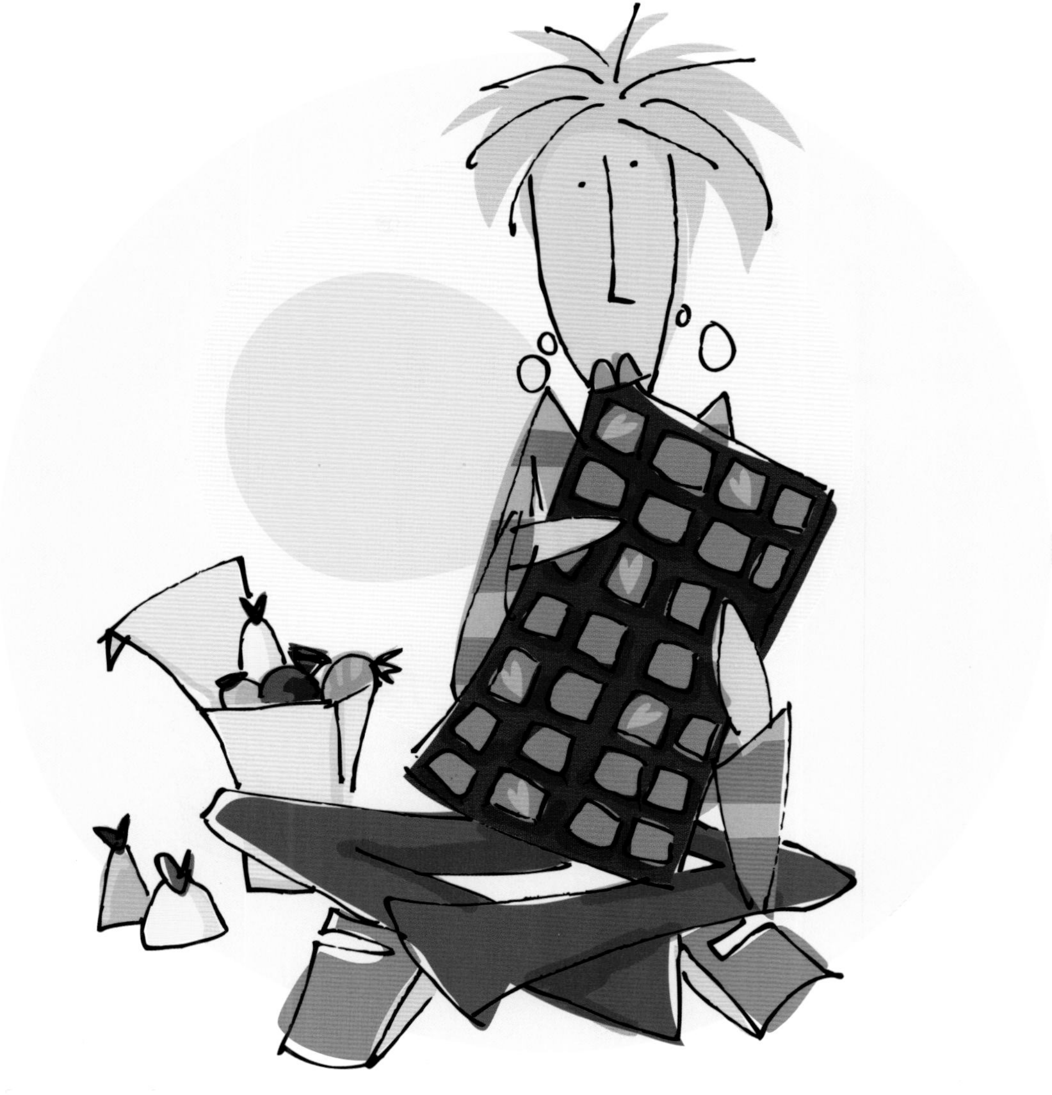

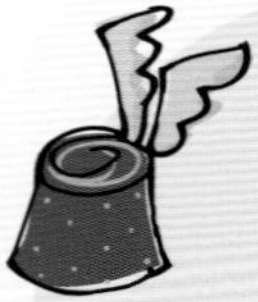

I never met a calorie I didn't like

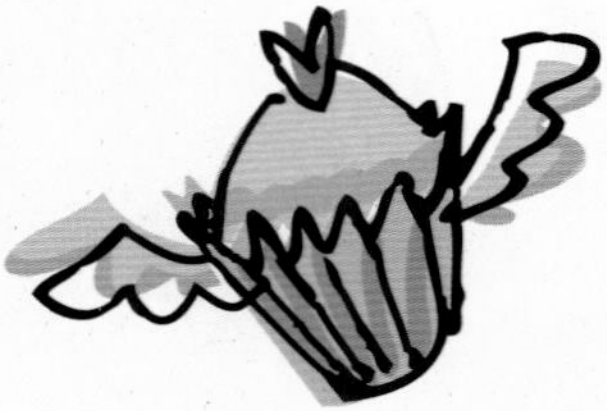

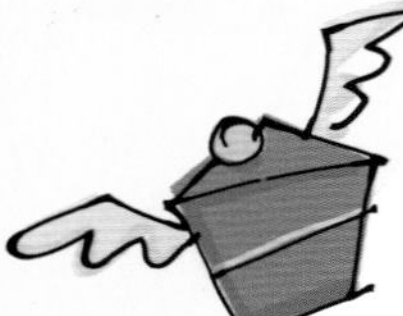

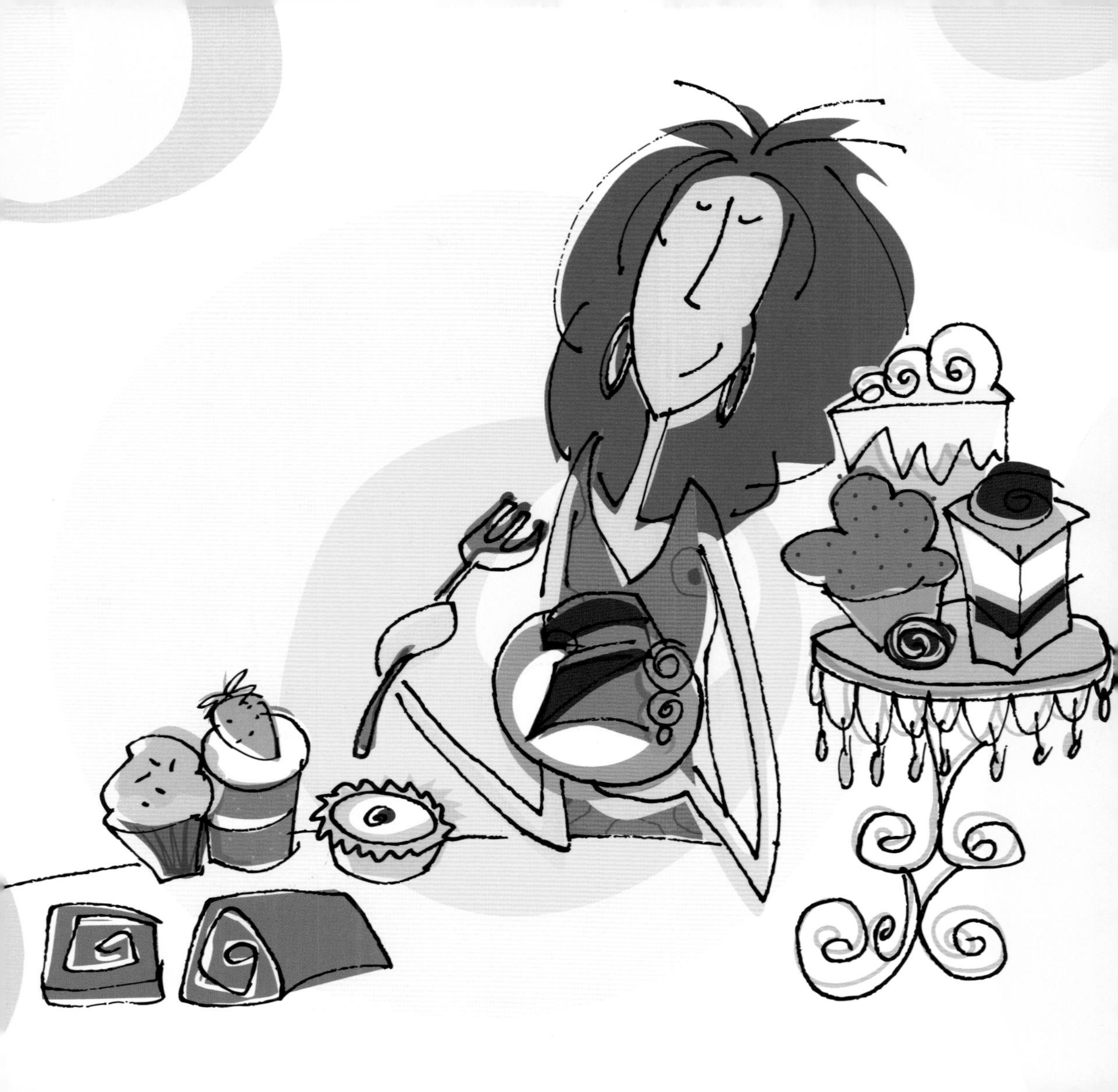

I try to watch
what I eat but
I'm not fast enough

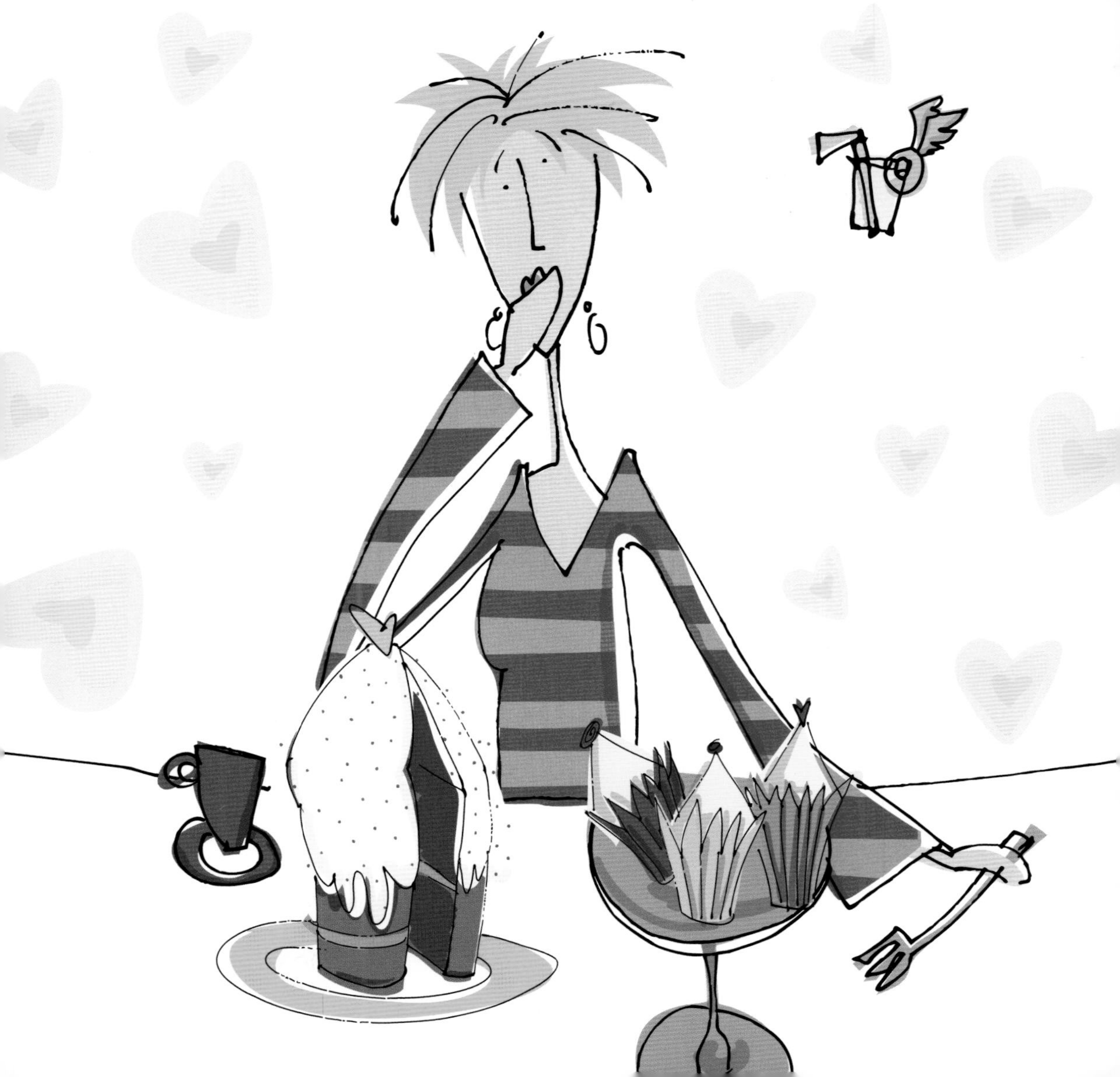

Man cannot live
by cake alone
but woman can

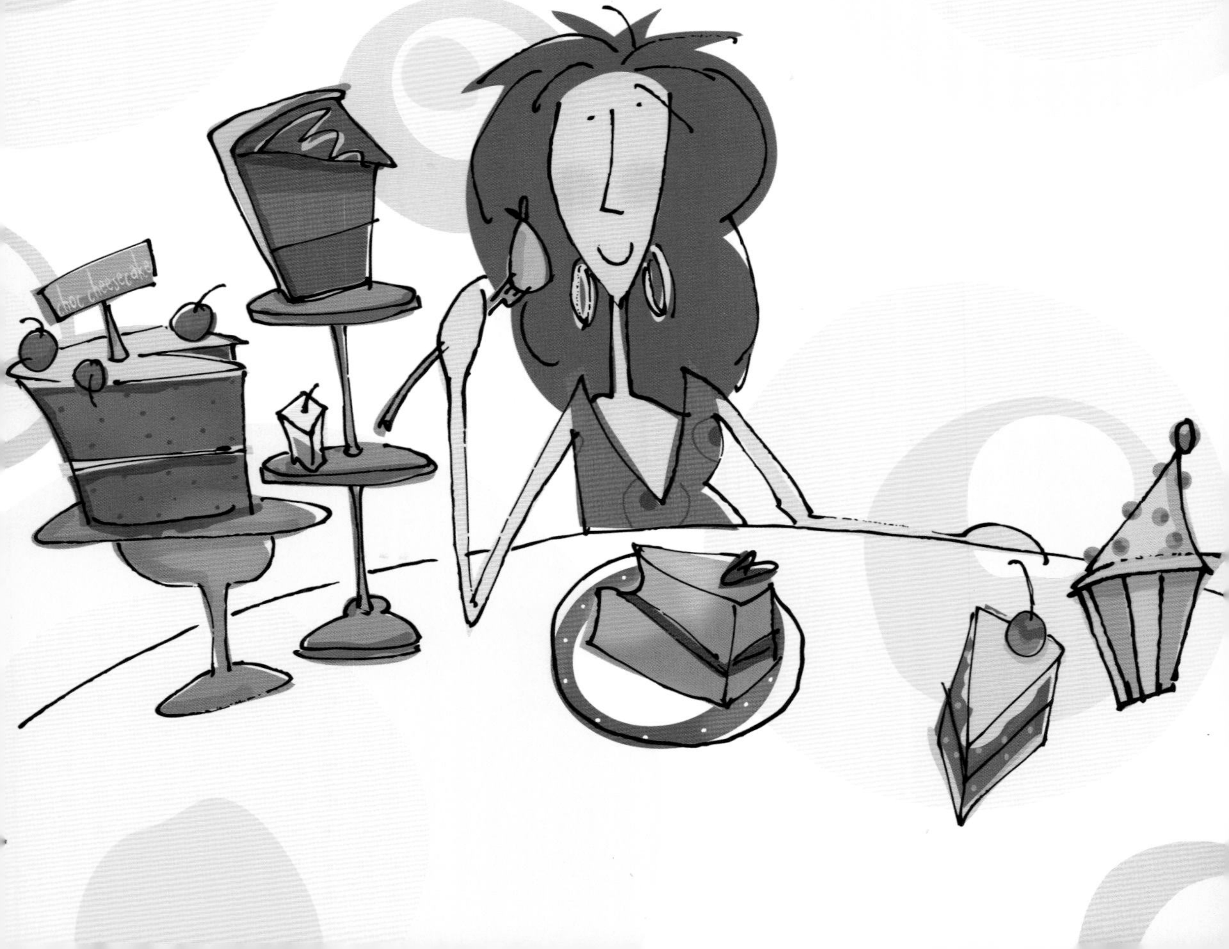
choc cheesecake

So much chocolate
so little time

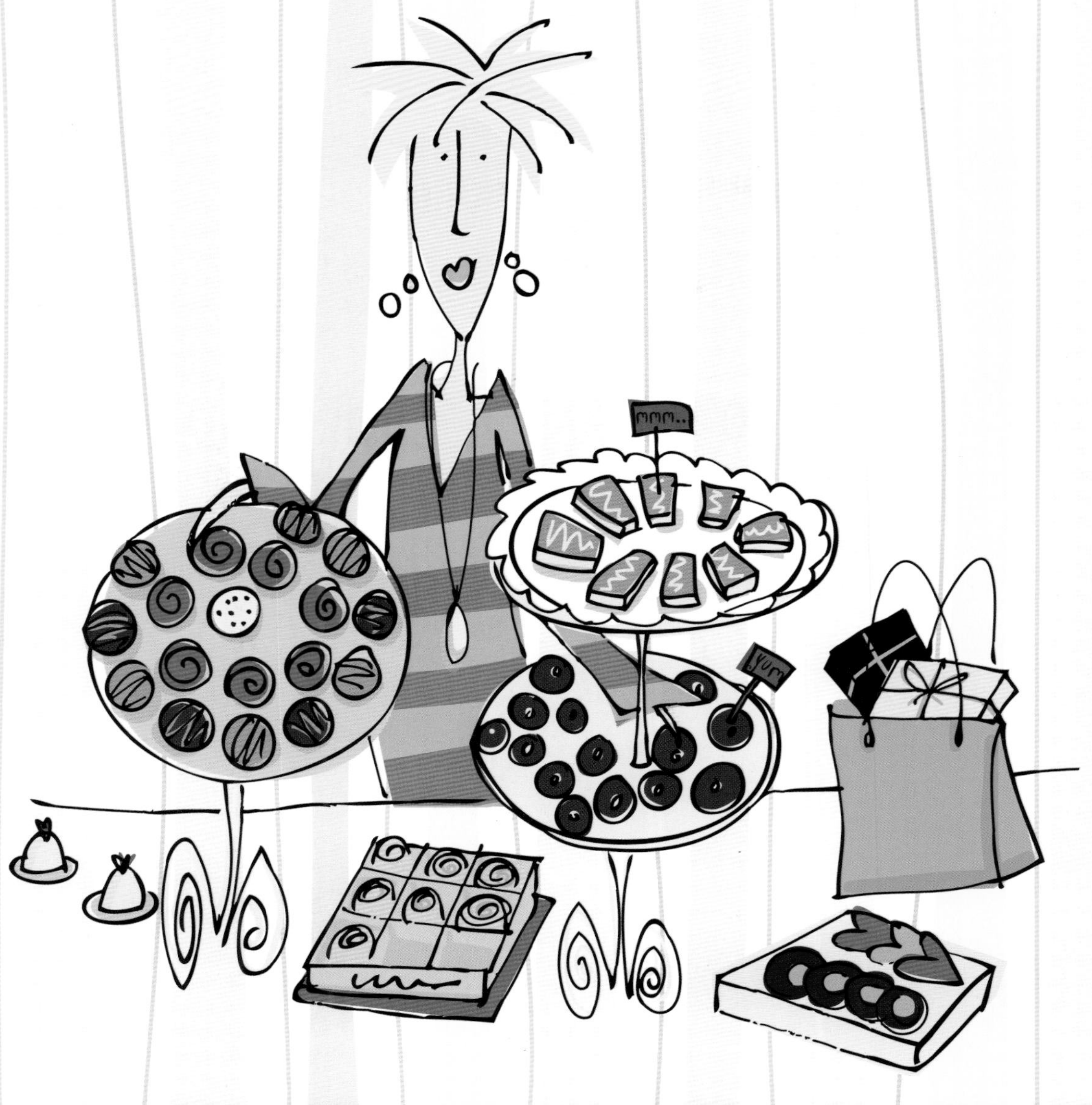
mmm...
yum

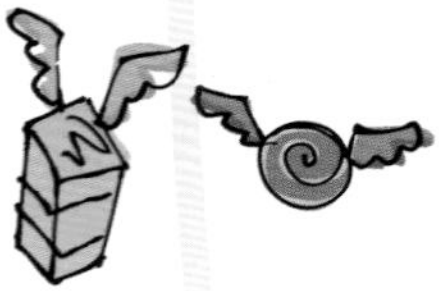

I no longer skinny dip
I chunky dunk

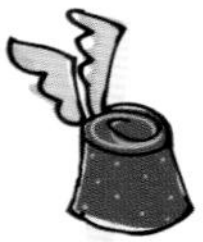

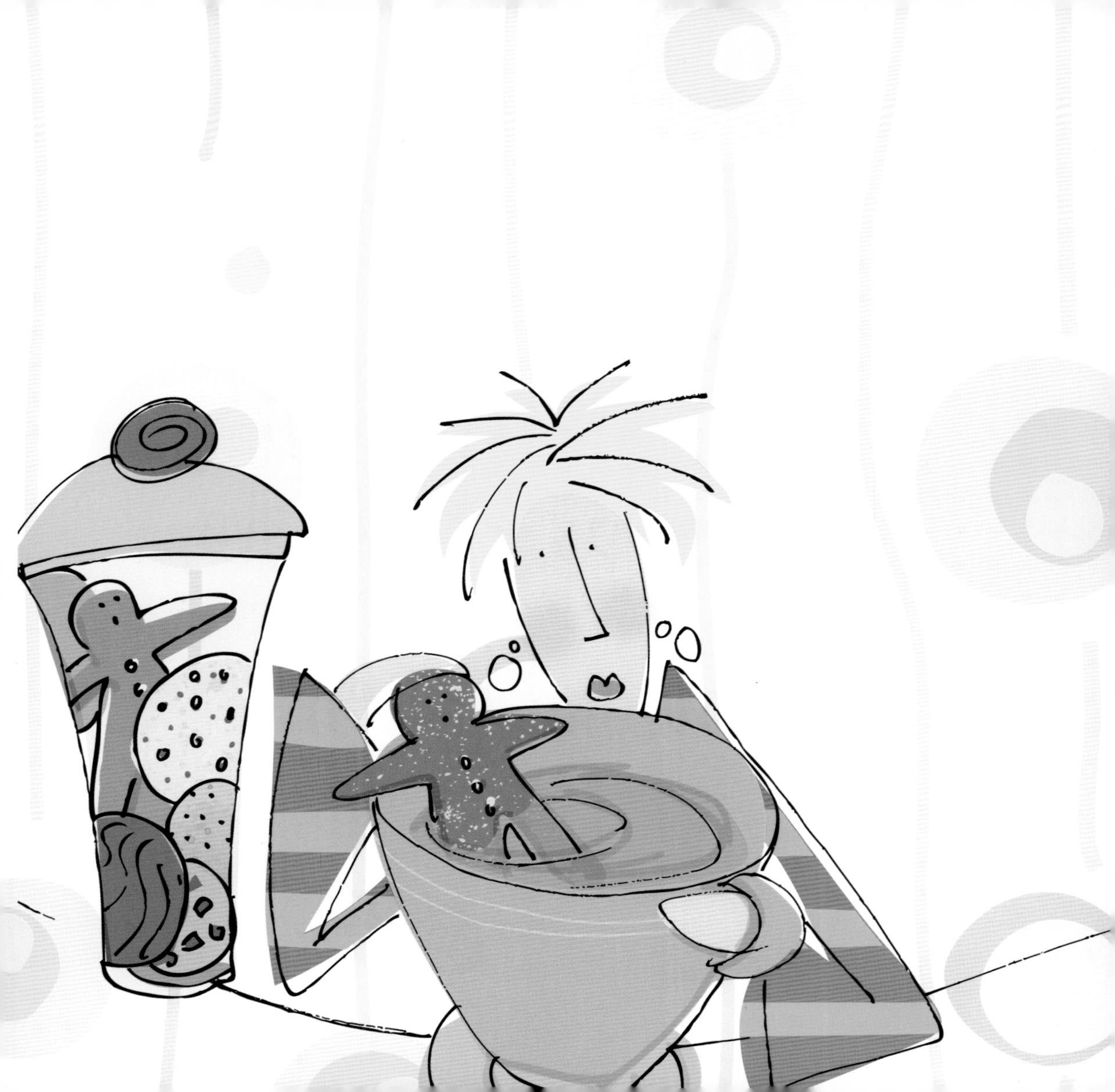

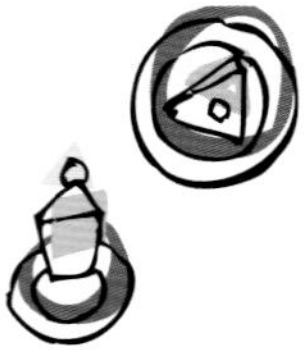

I eat all the main food groups, microwave, fast and frozen

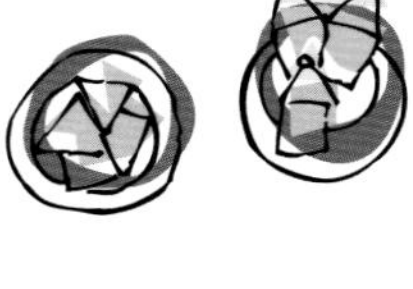

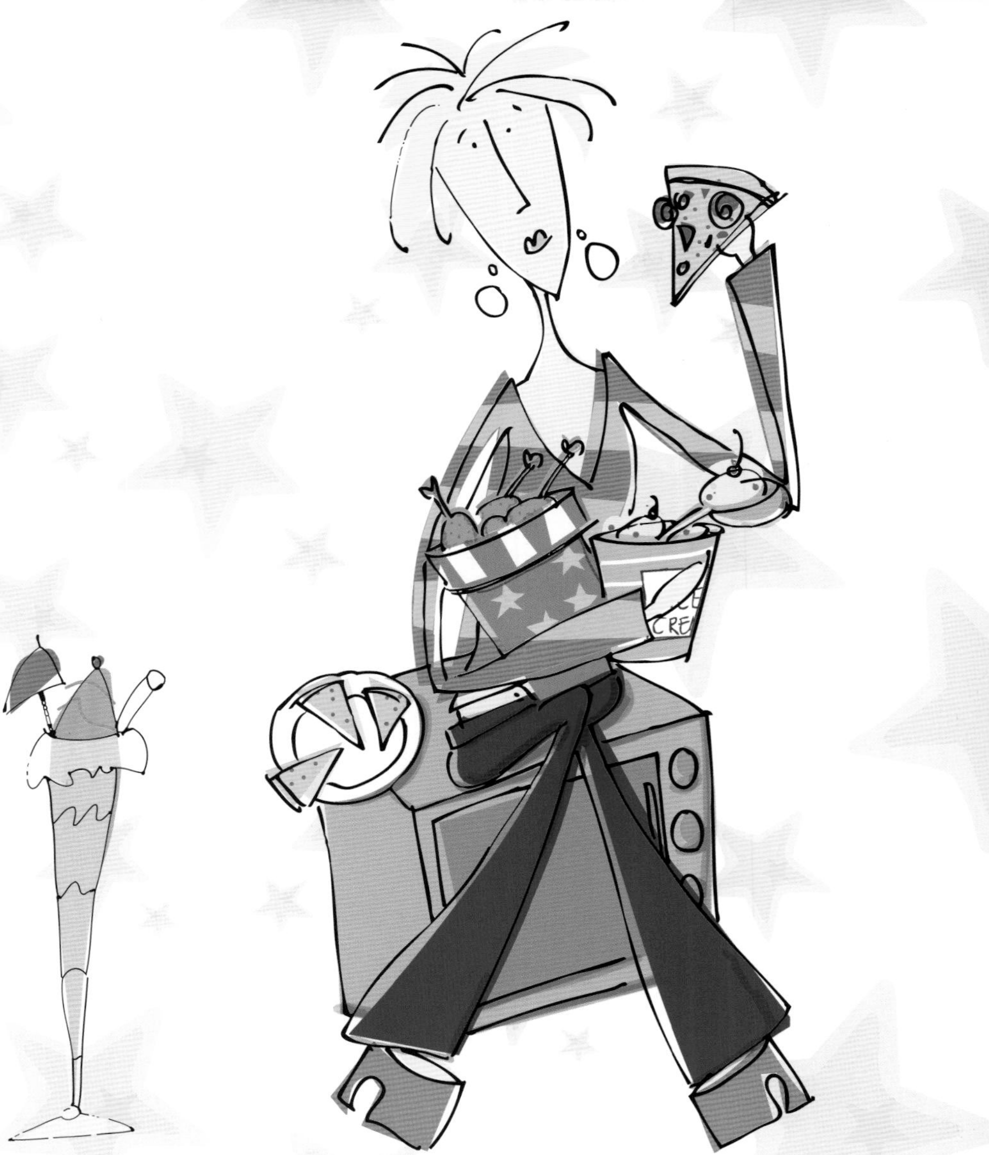

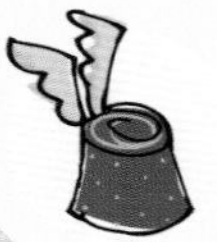

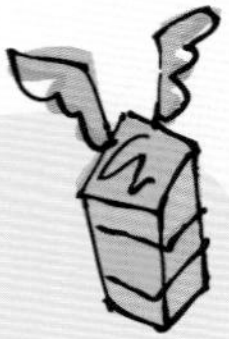

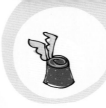

Lead me not into temptation, I can find the way myself

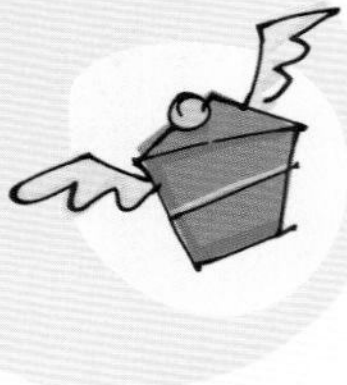

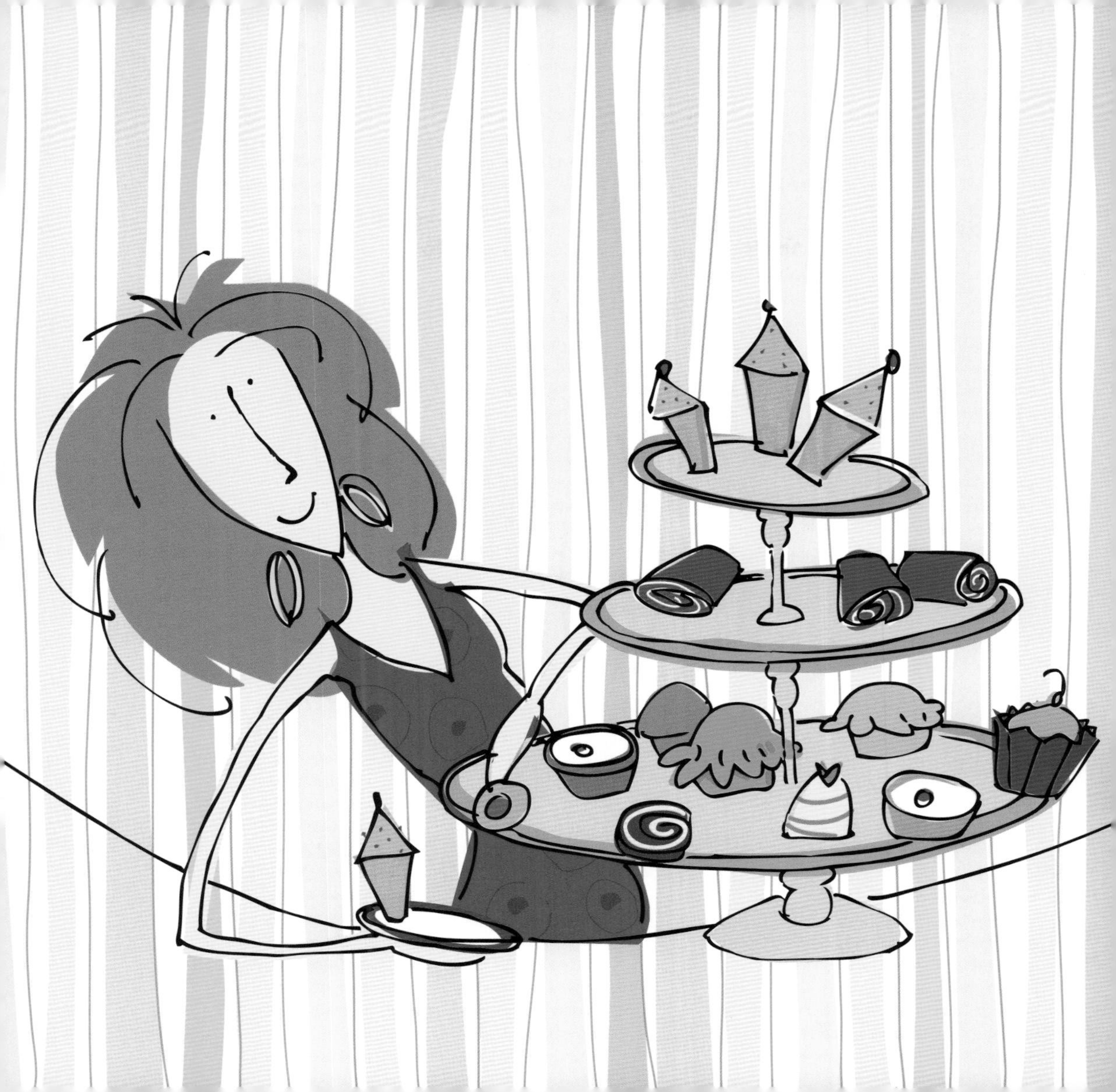

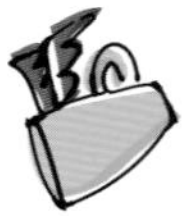

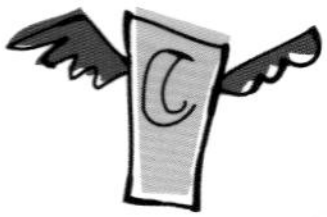

We've got to stop eating like this

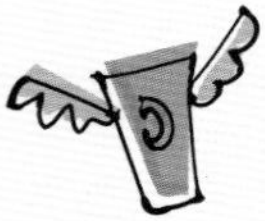

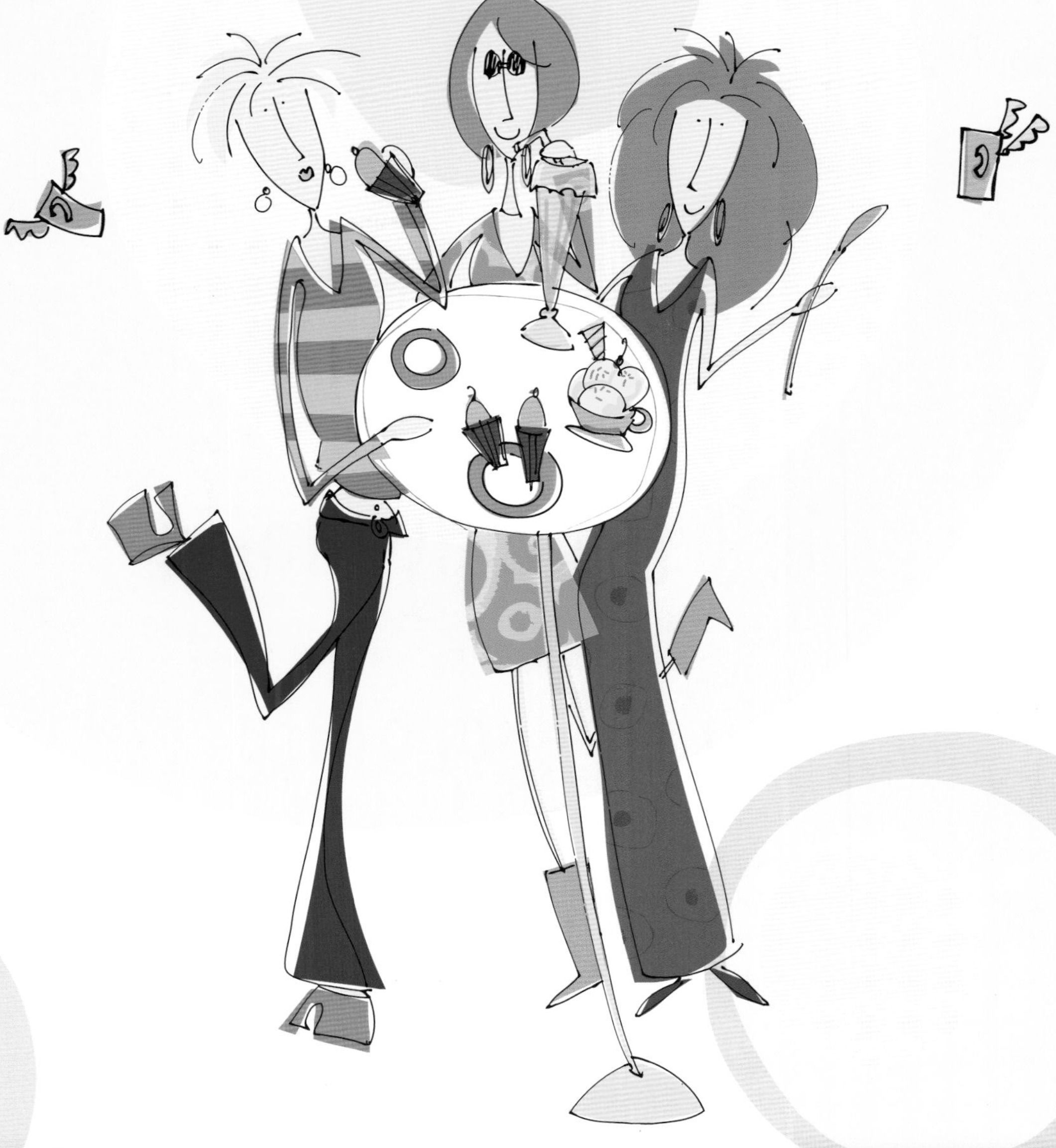

Save the Earth,
it's the only planet
with chocolate

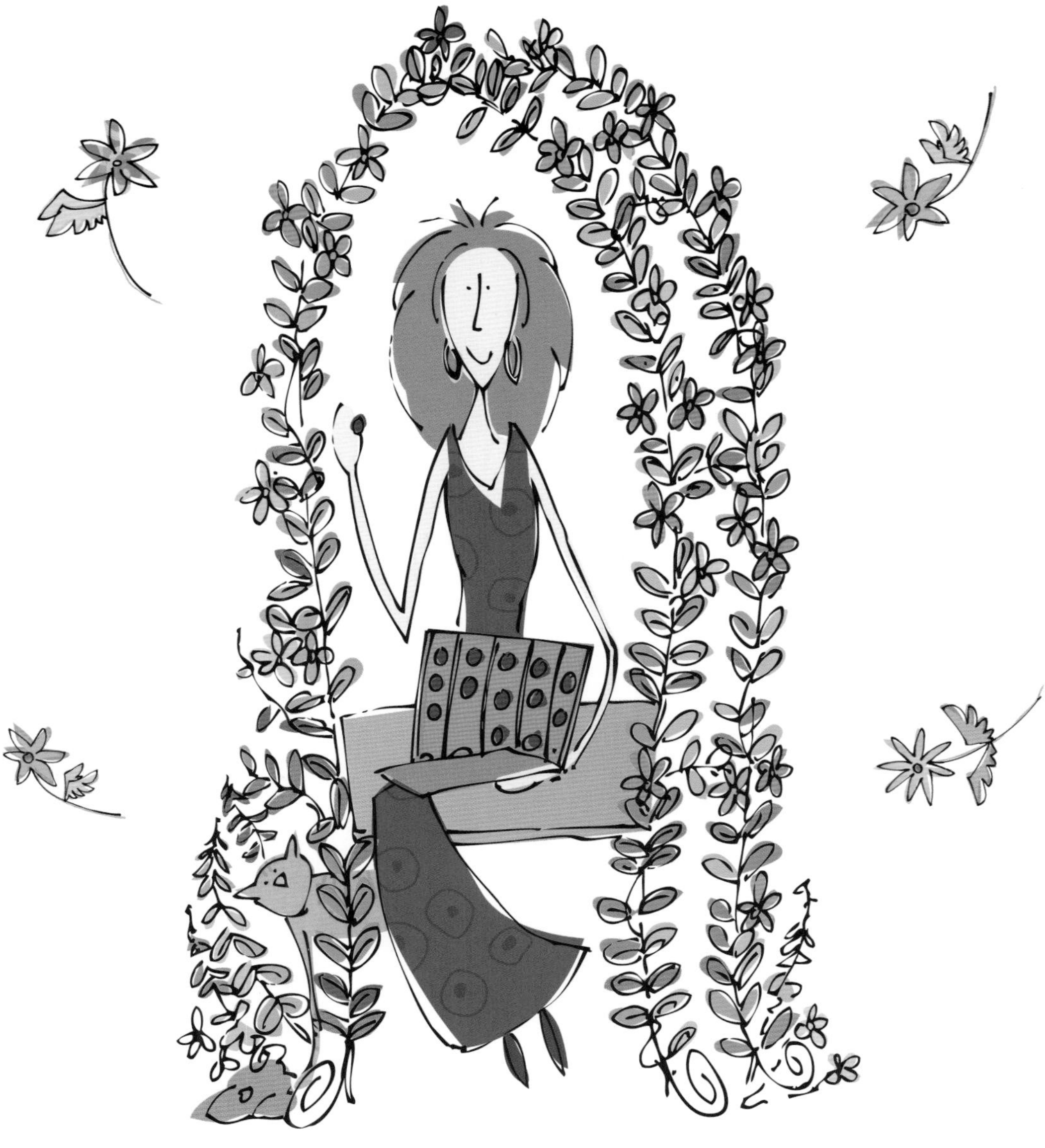

Some things are
worth the weight

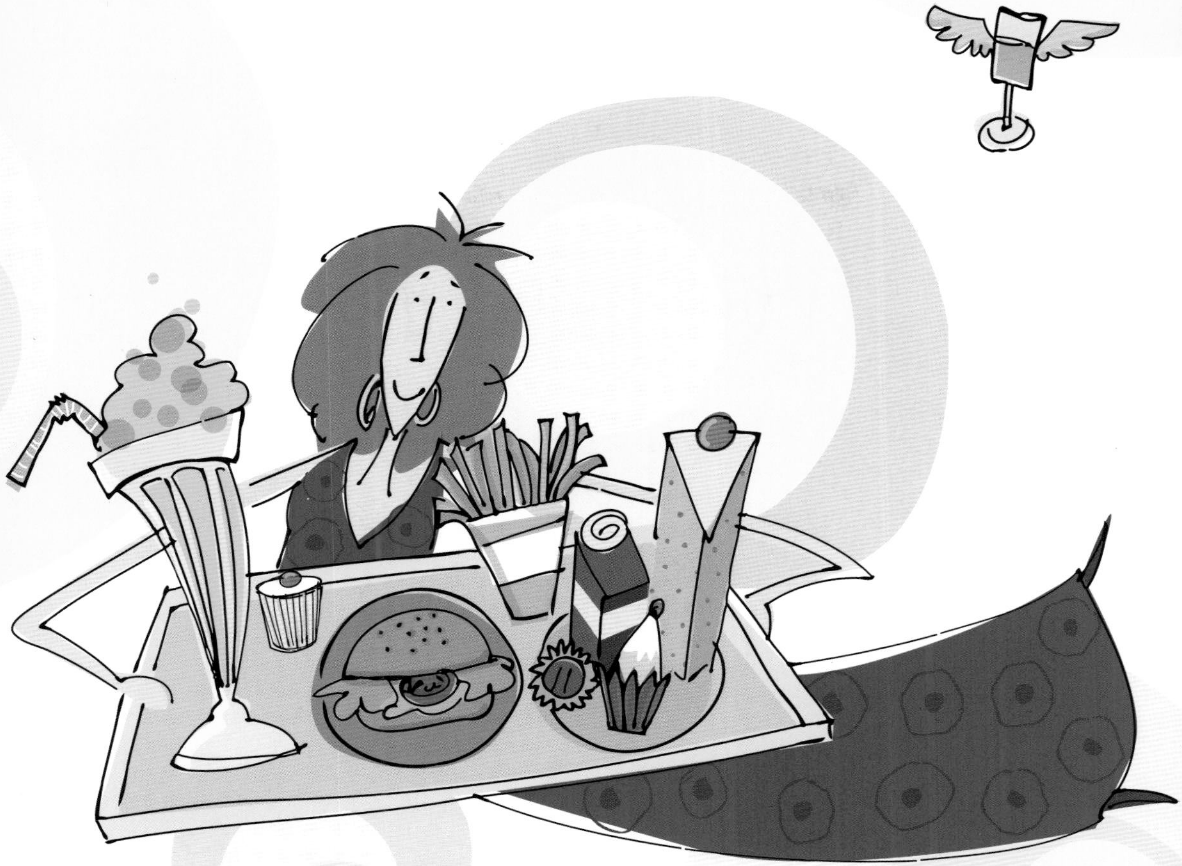

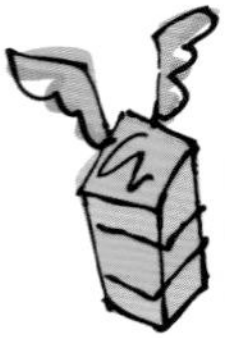

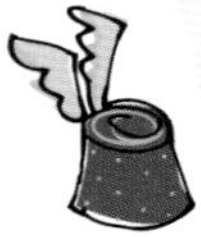

A balanced diet is a cookie in each hand

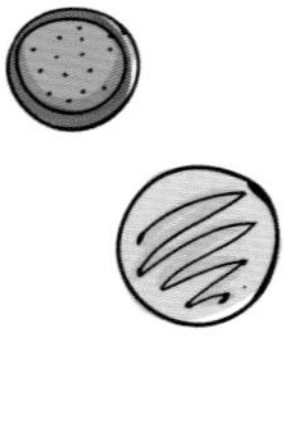

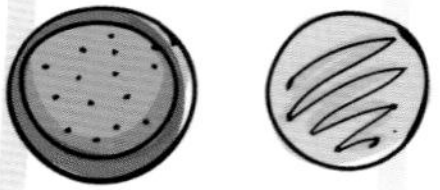

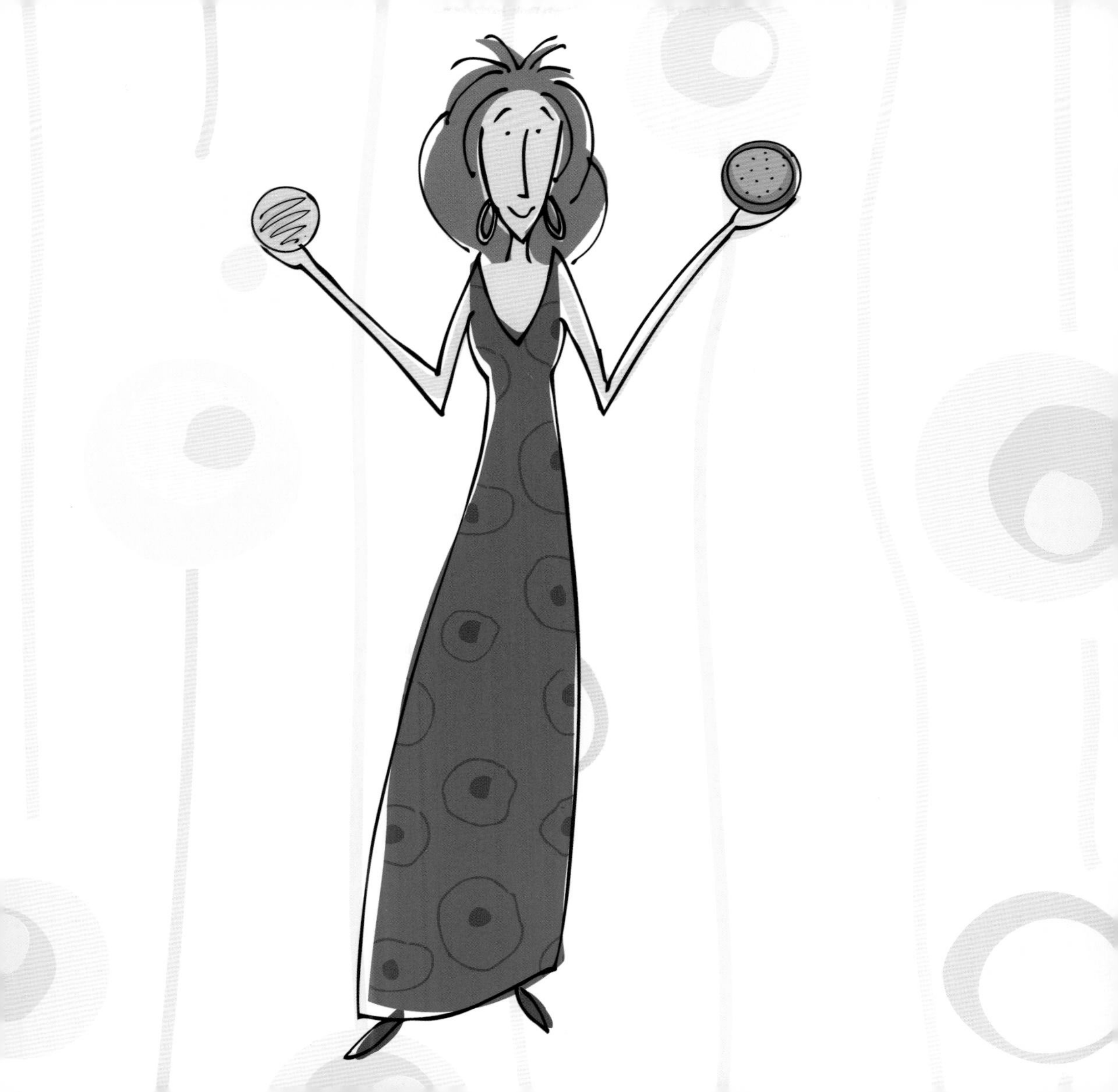

Exercise is a dirty word...
...every time I hear it,
I wash my mouth out
with chocolate

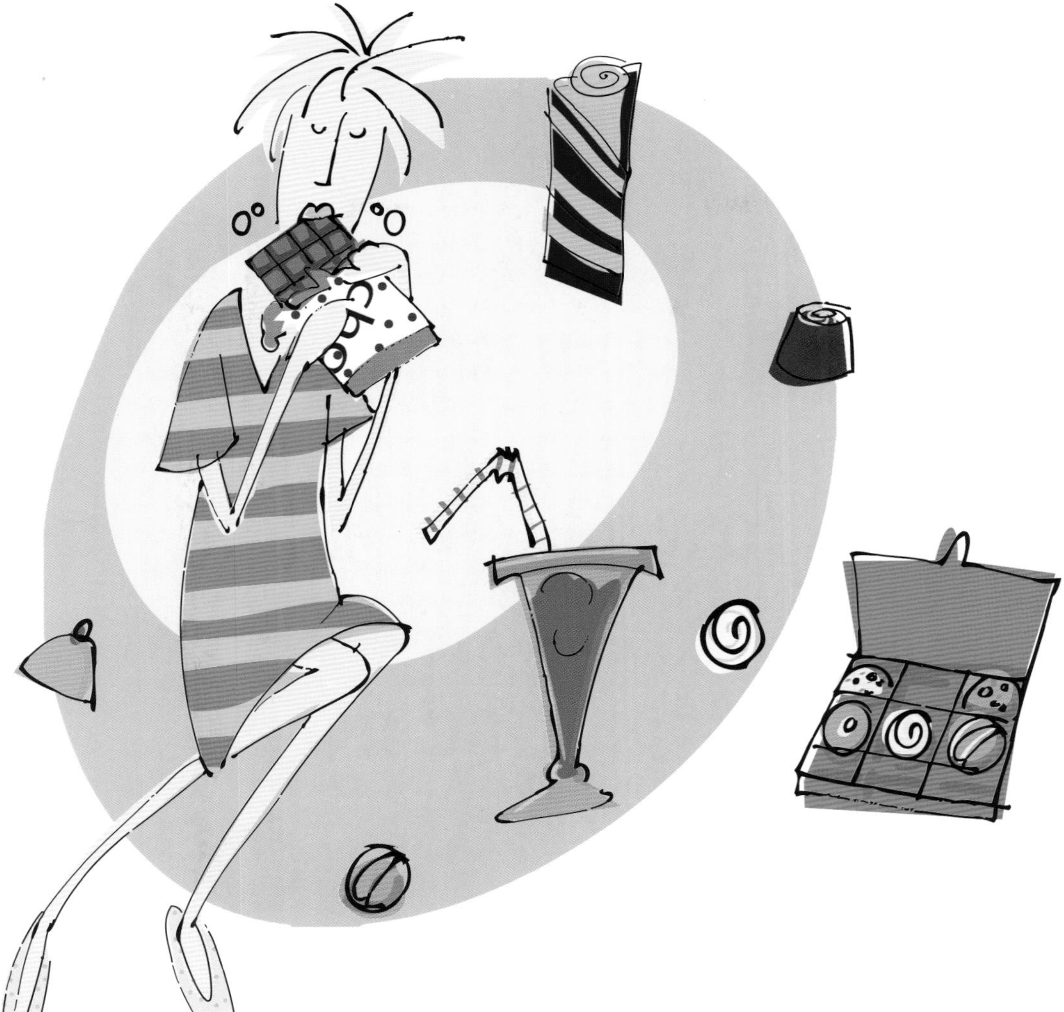

I keep trying to lose weight but it keeps finding me

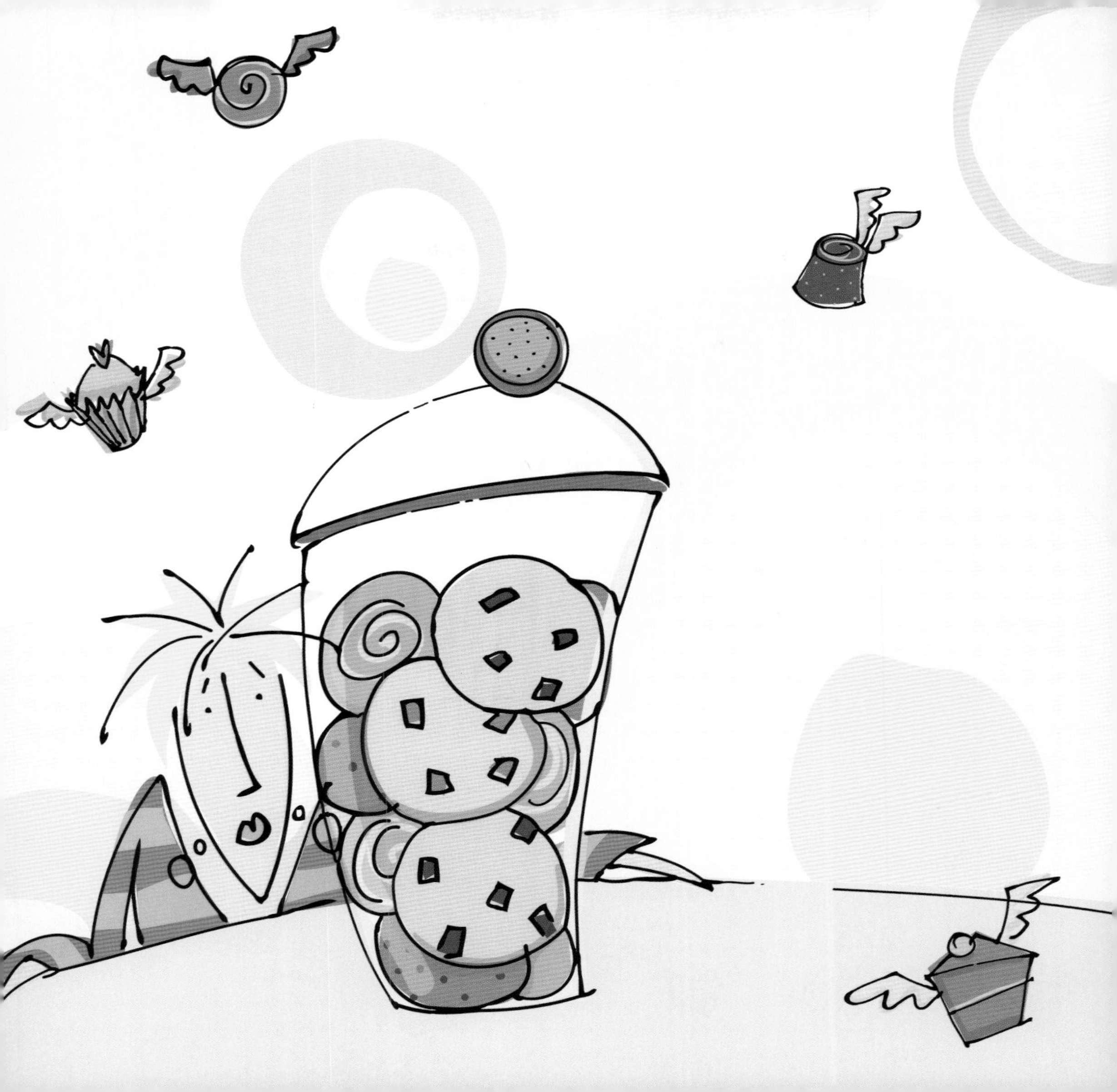

Dieting is
wishful shrinking

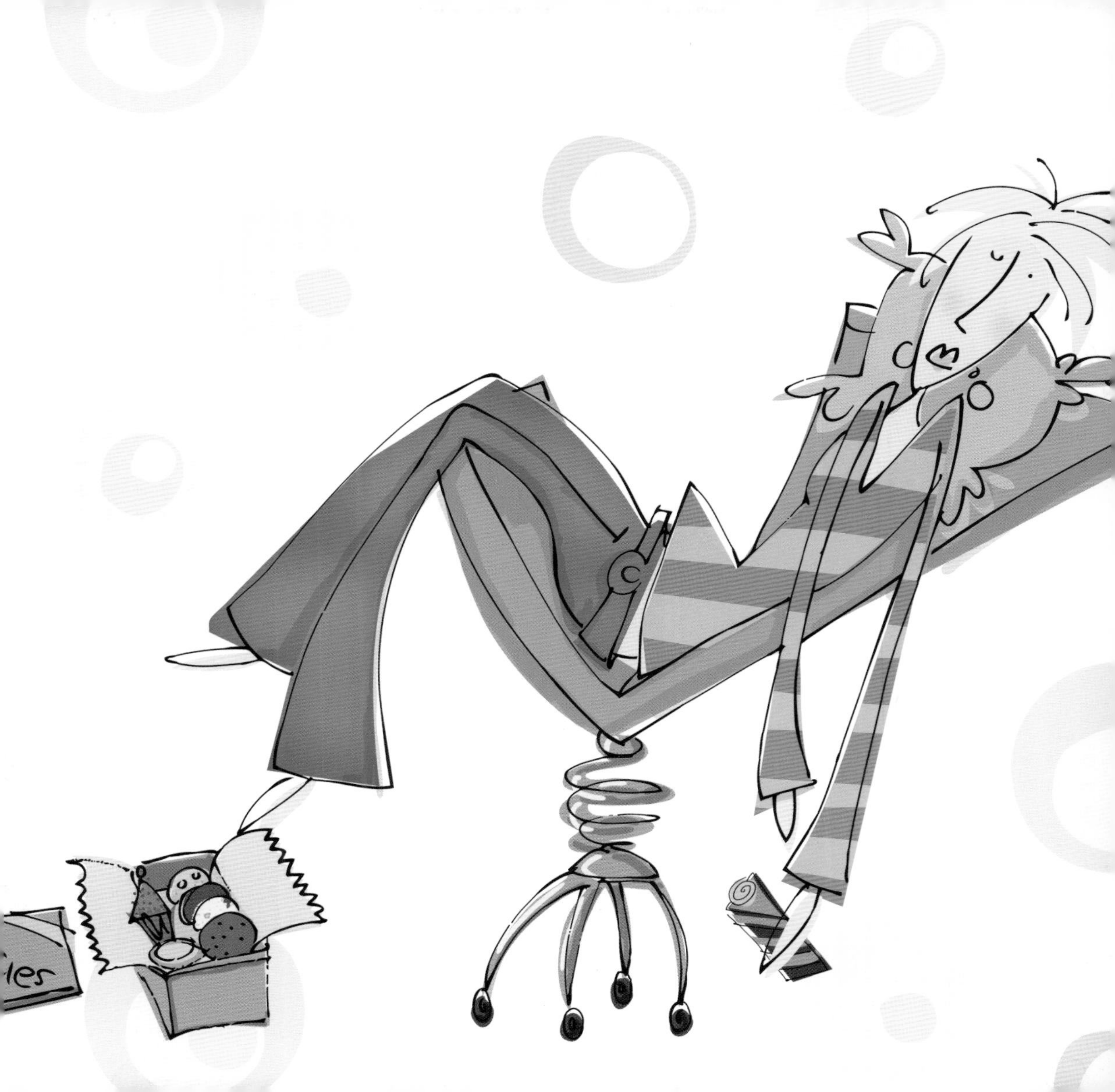

How can I diet...
the fridge is still full!

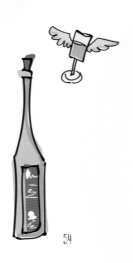

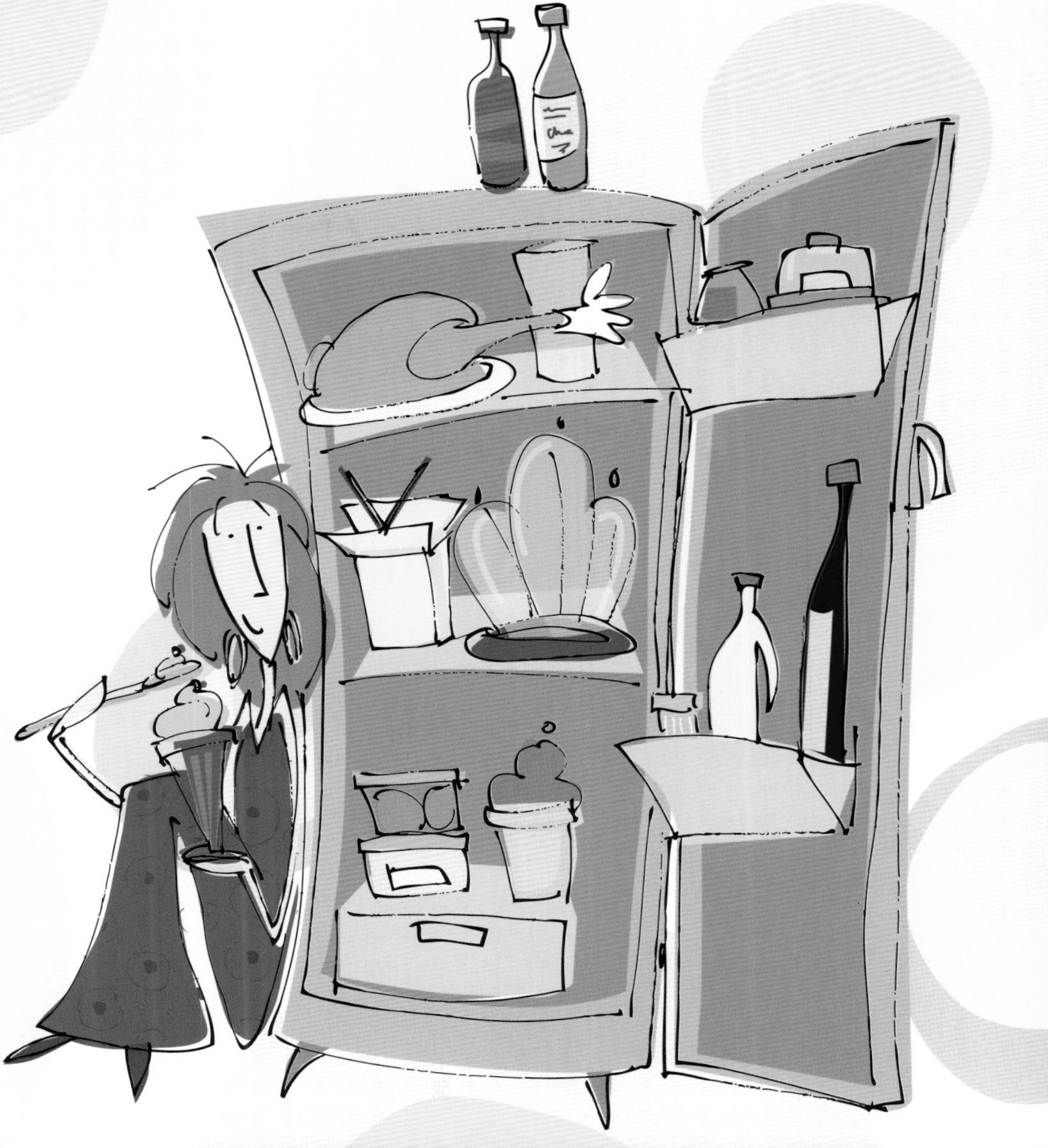

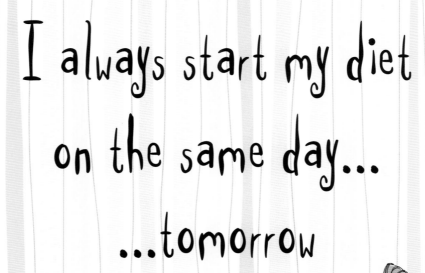

I always start my diet
on the same day...
...tomorrow

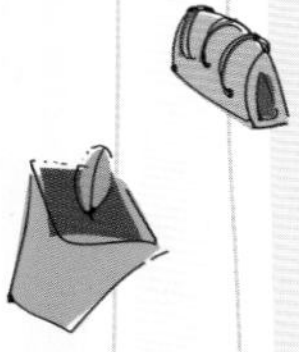

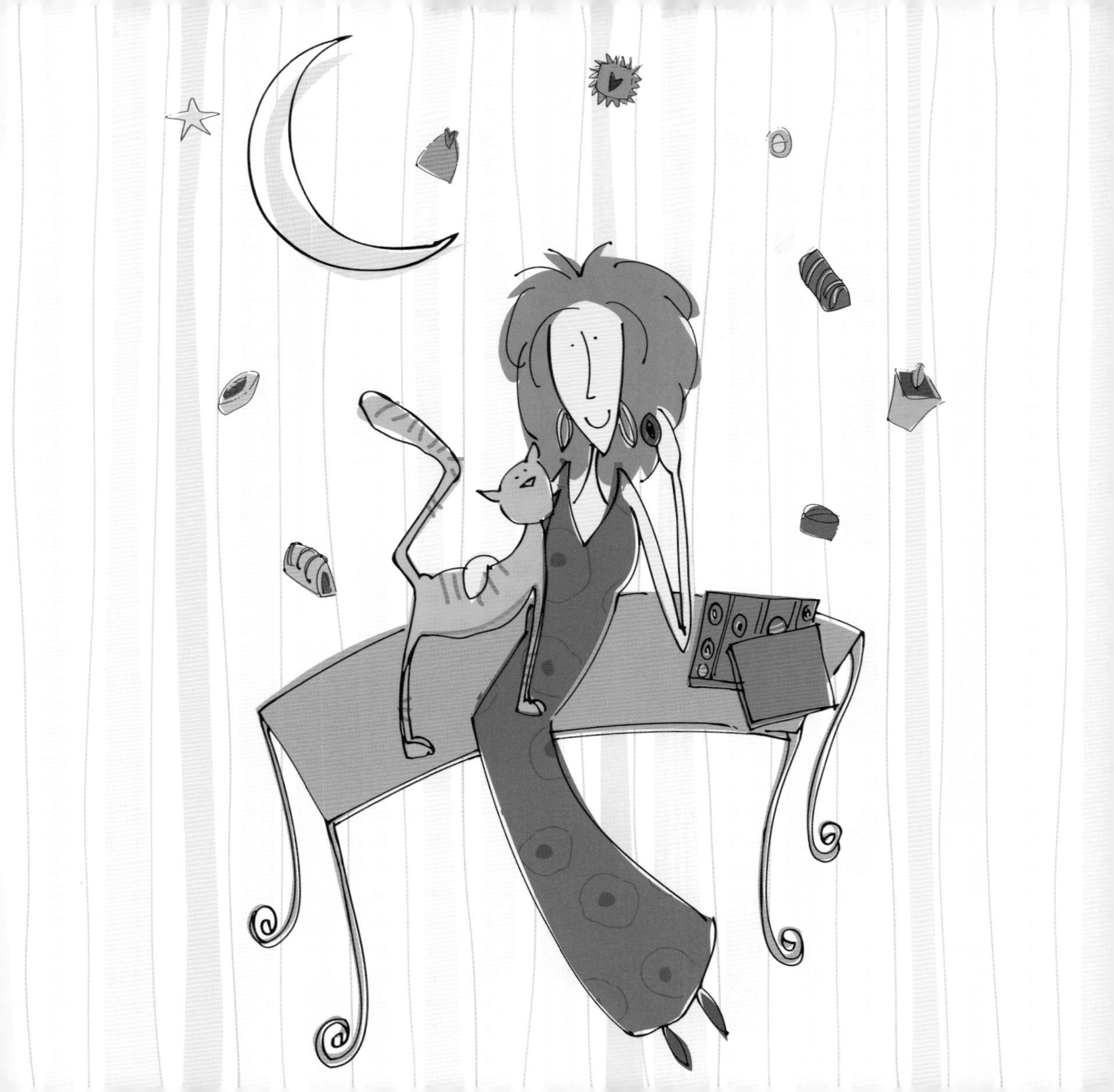

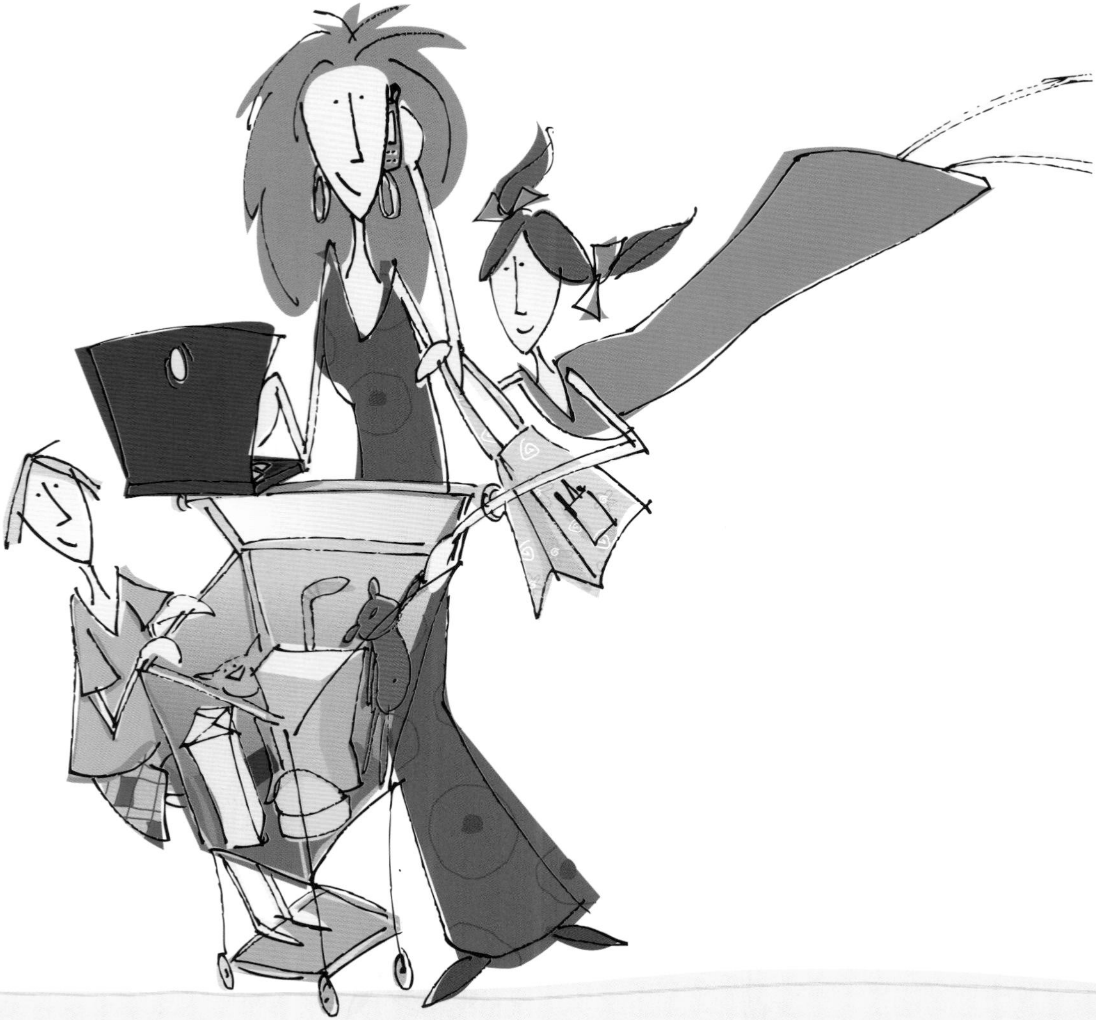

Born to be a
Yummy Mummy

We childproofed the house... but they keep getting in

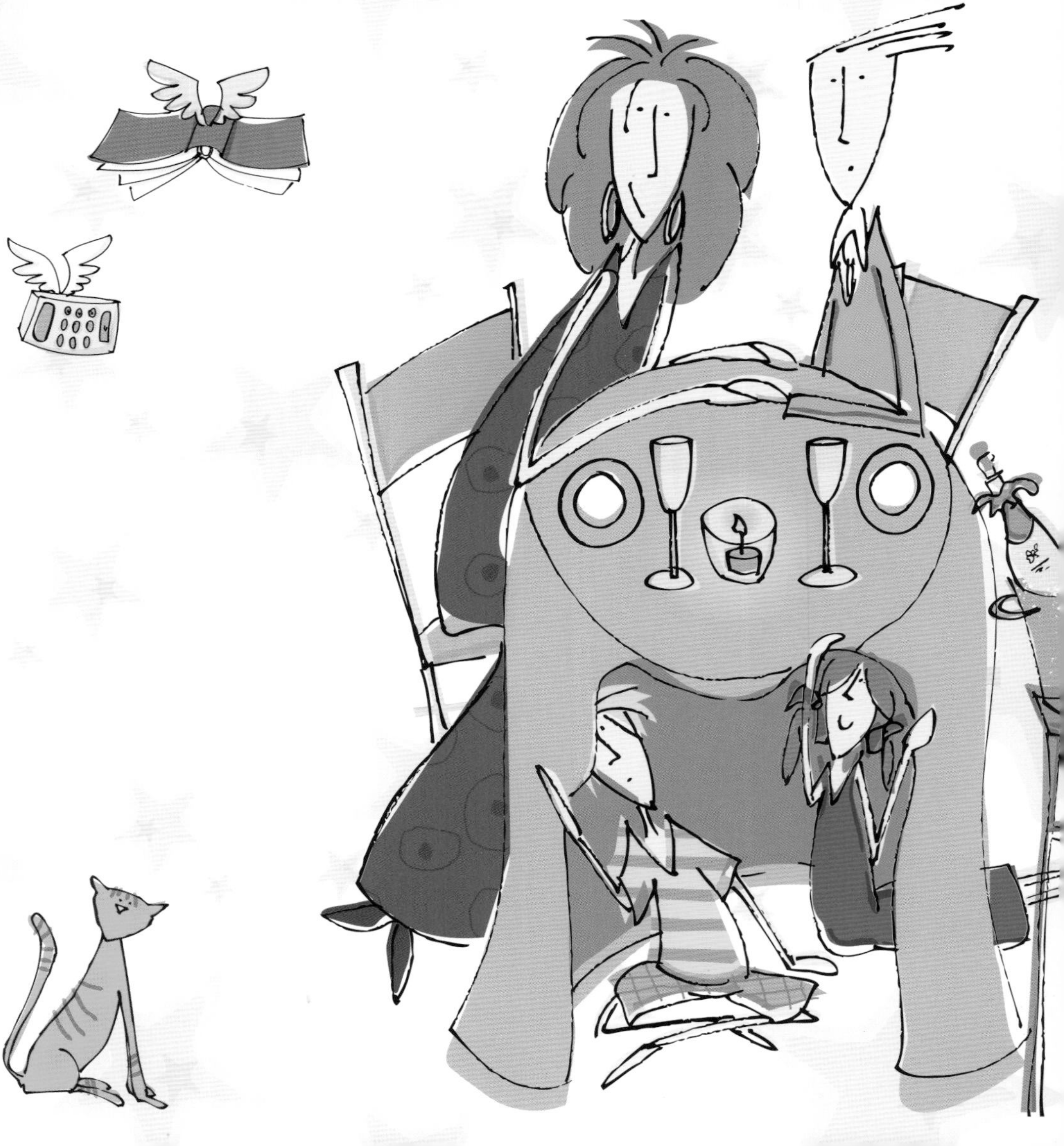

'M' is for Mother,
not for Maid

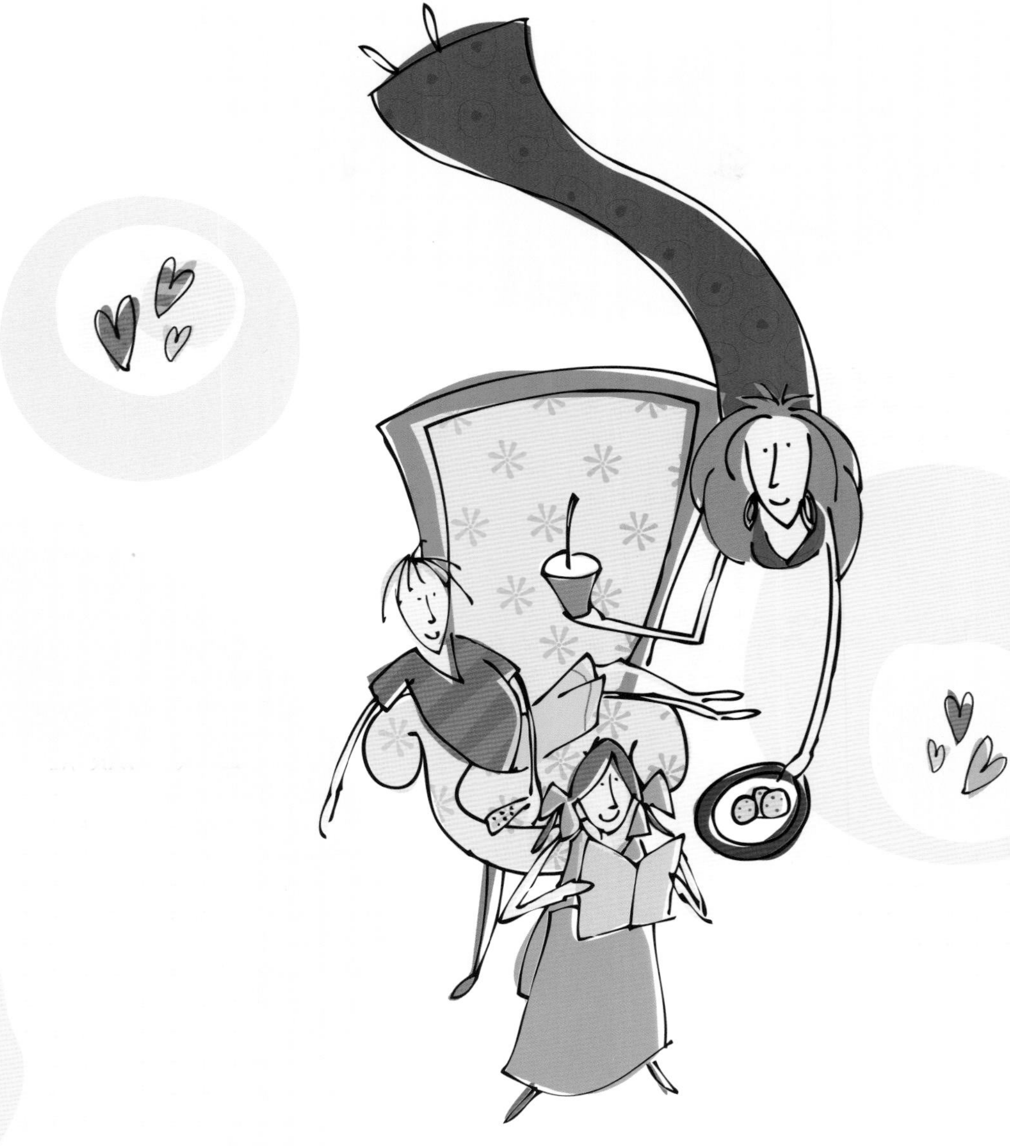

If a mother's place
is in the home,
why am I always
in the car!

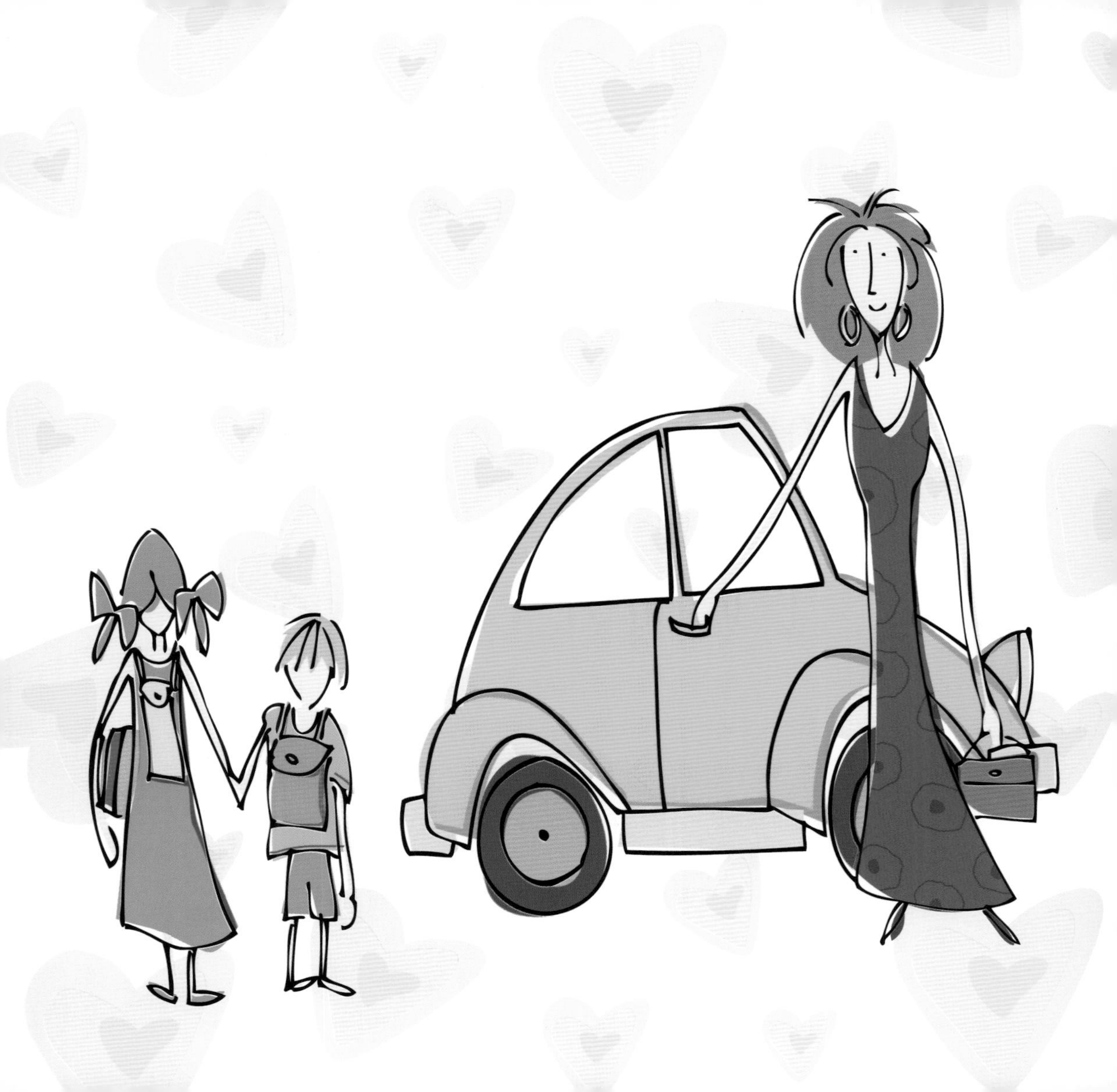

You don't scare me,
I've got children

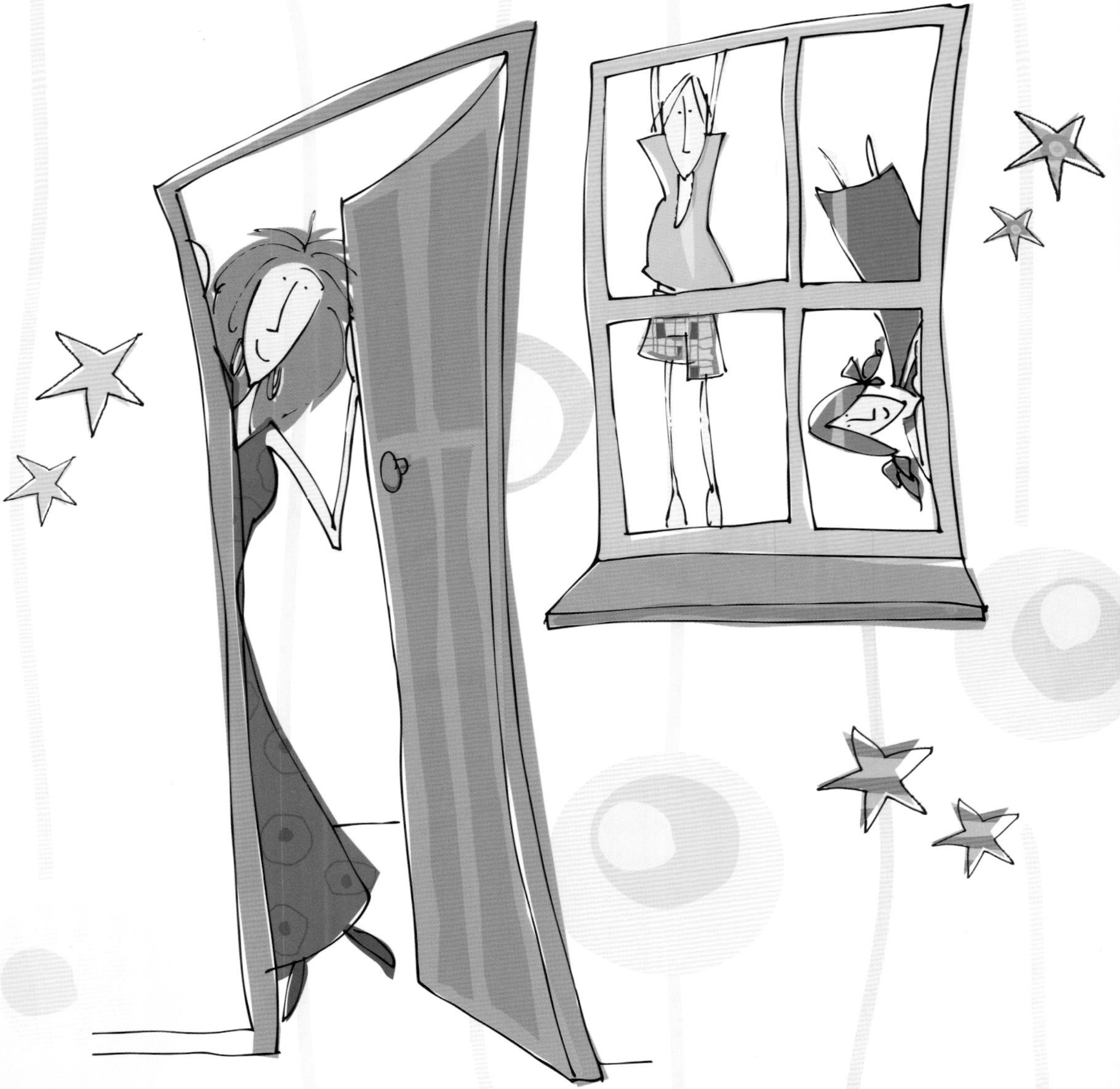

Mothers of little boys work from son up to son down

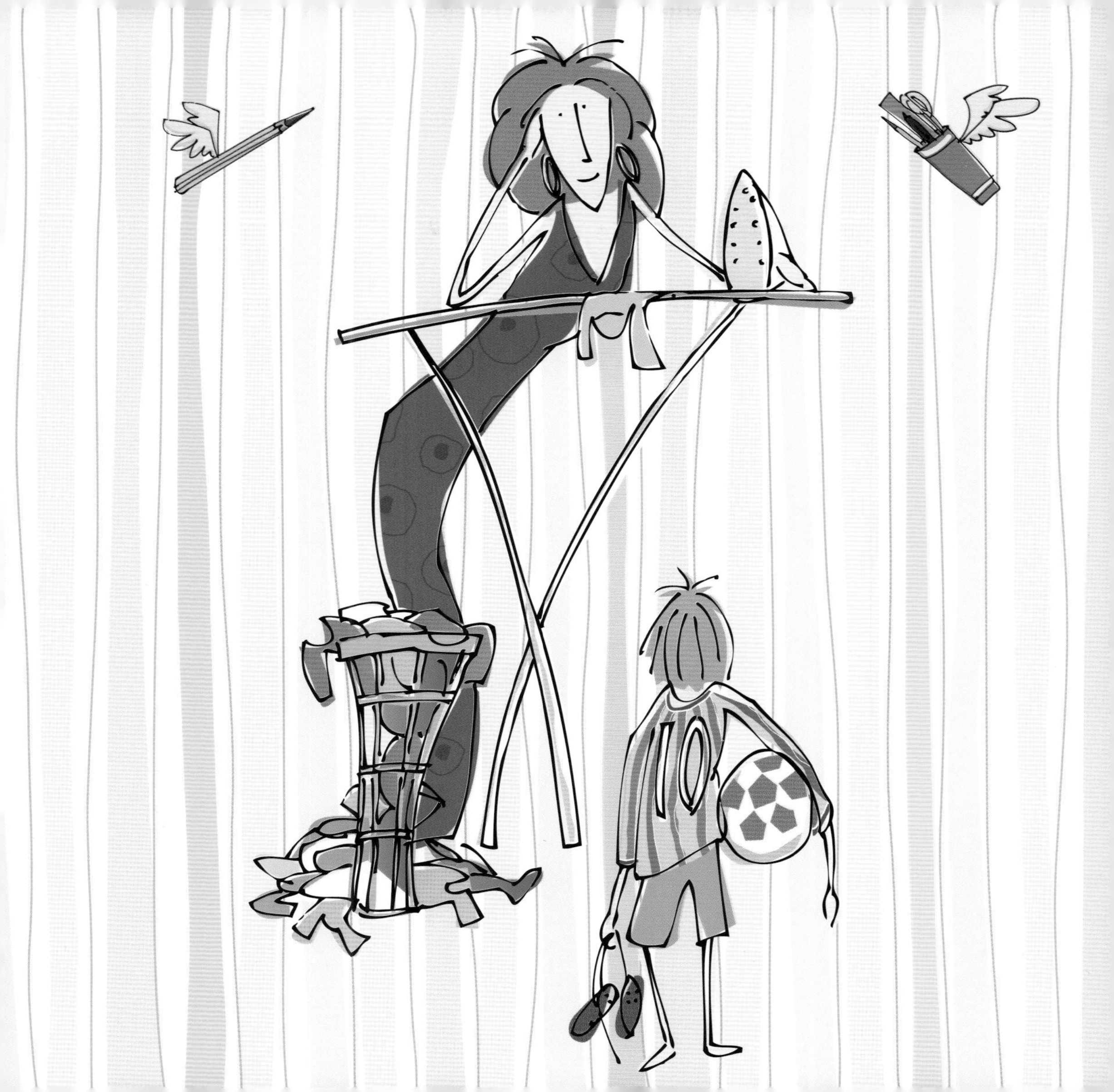
10

Mothers hold their children's hands a while, and their hearts forever

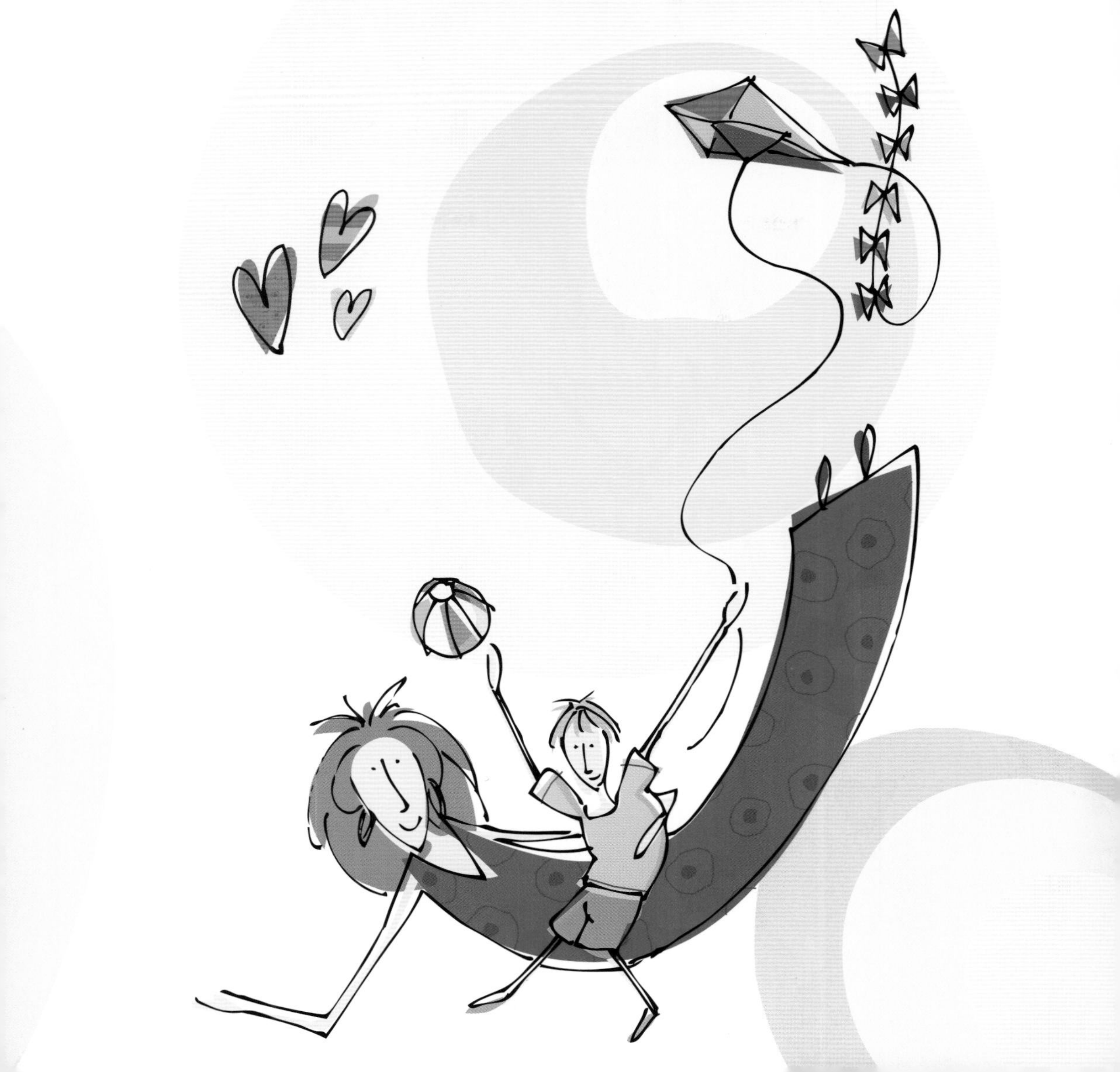

So it's not
home sweet home...
adjust!

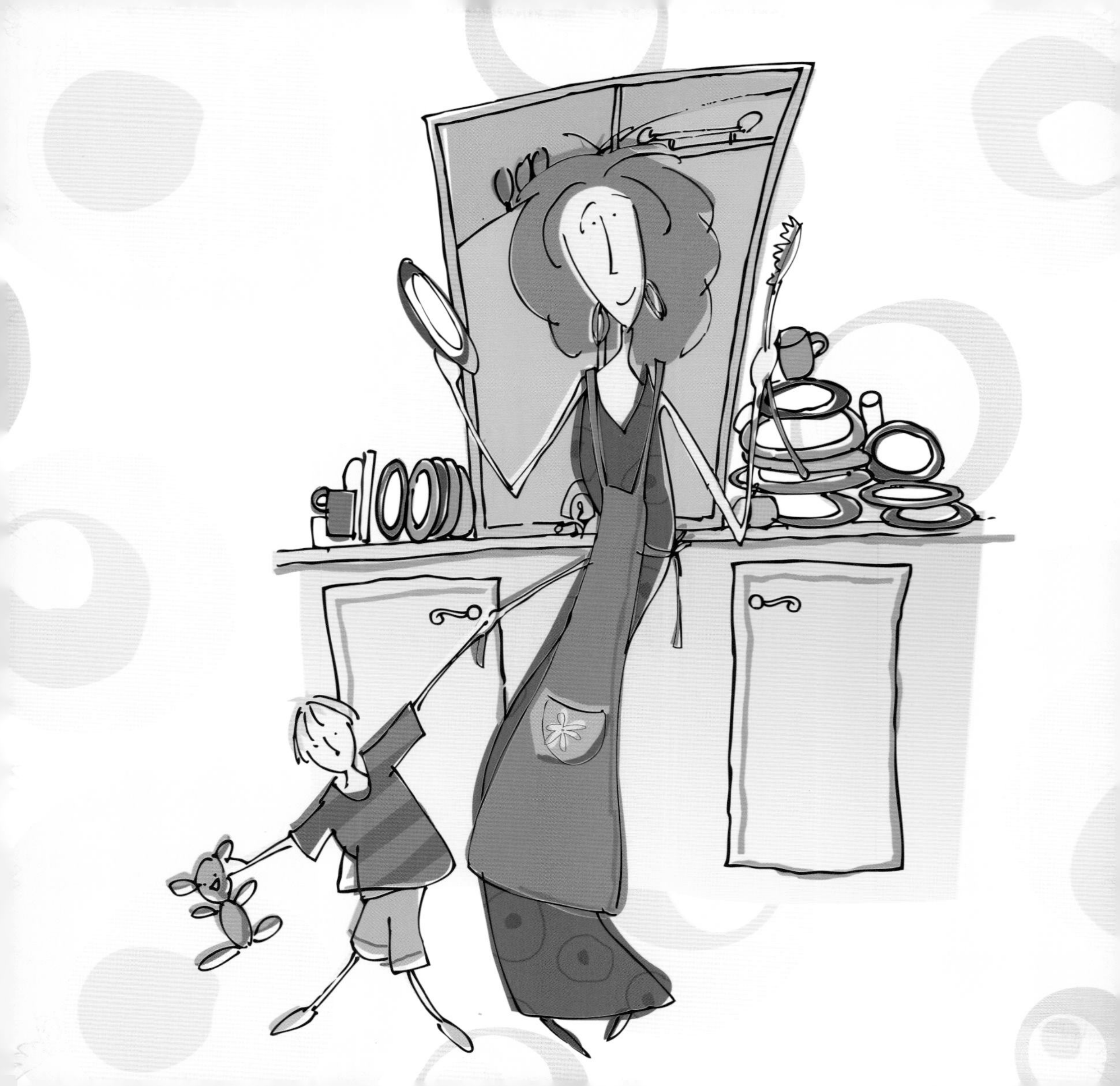

My family tree
is full of nuts

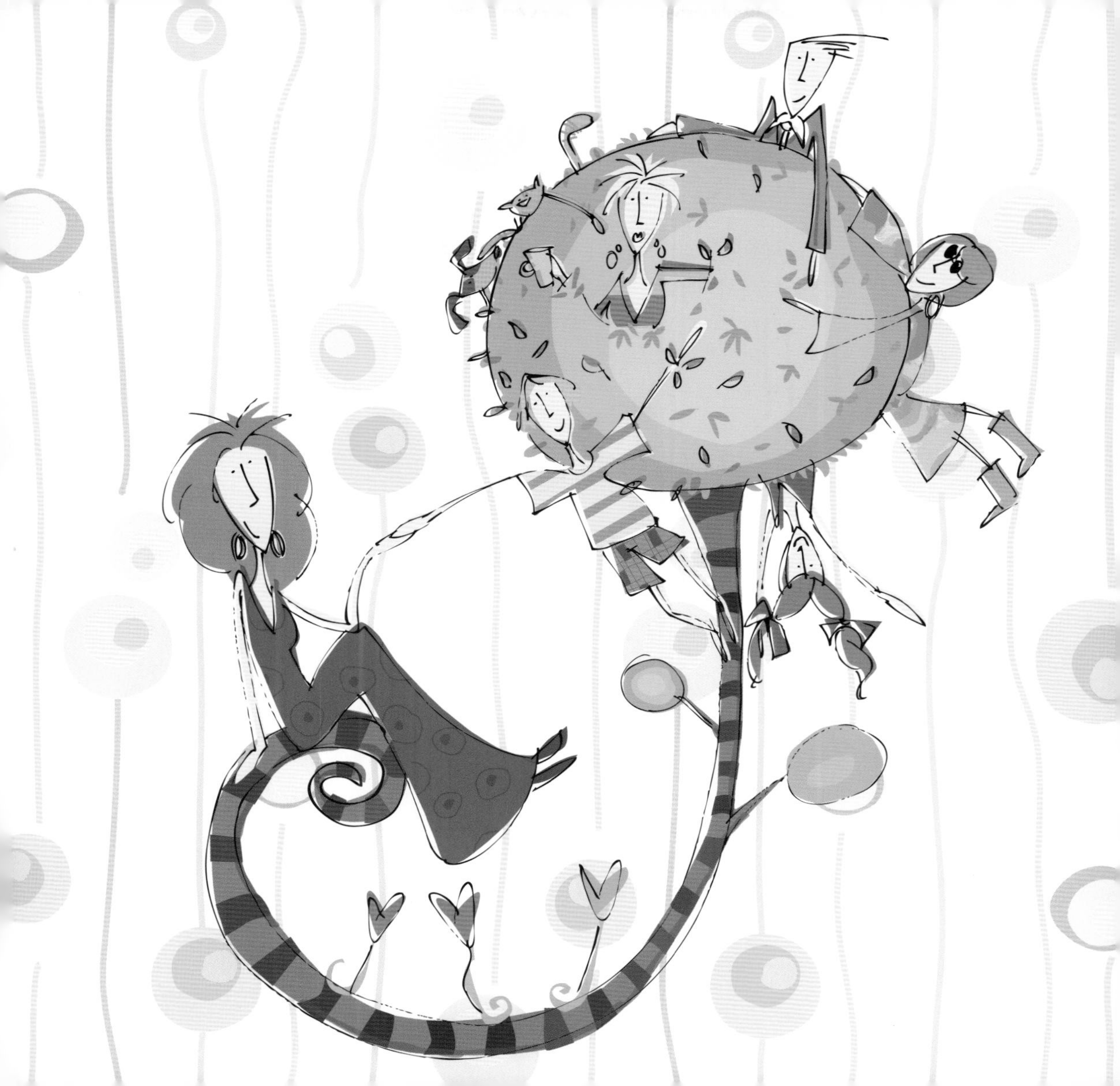

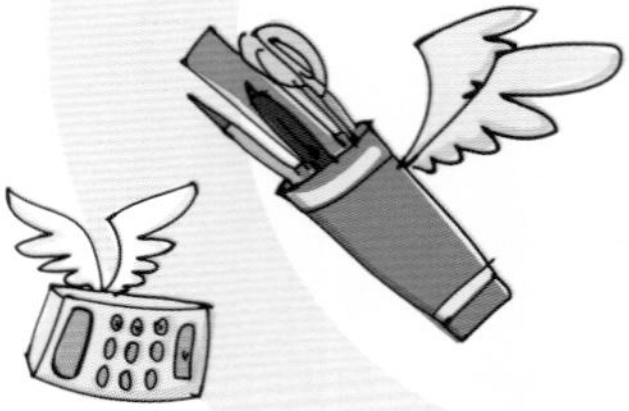

Brain still loading... please wait

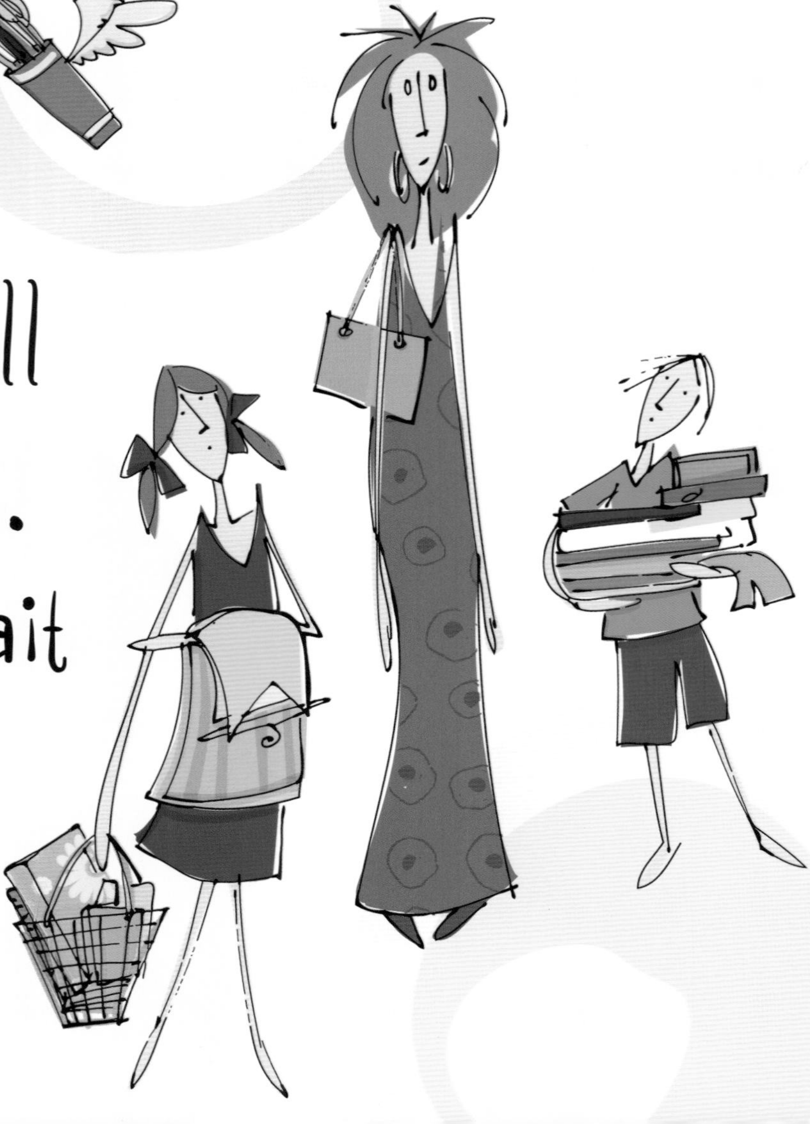

Mums are like buttons
they hold
things together

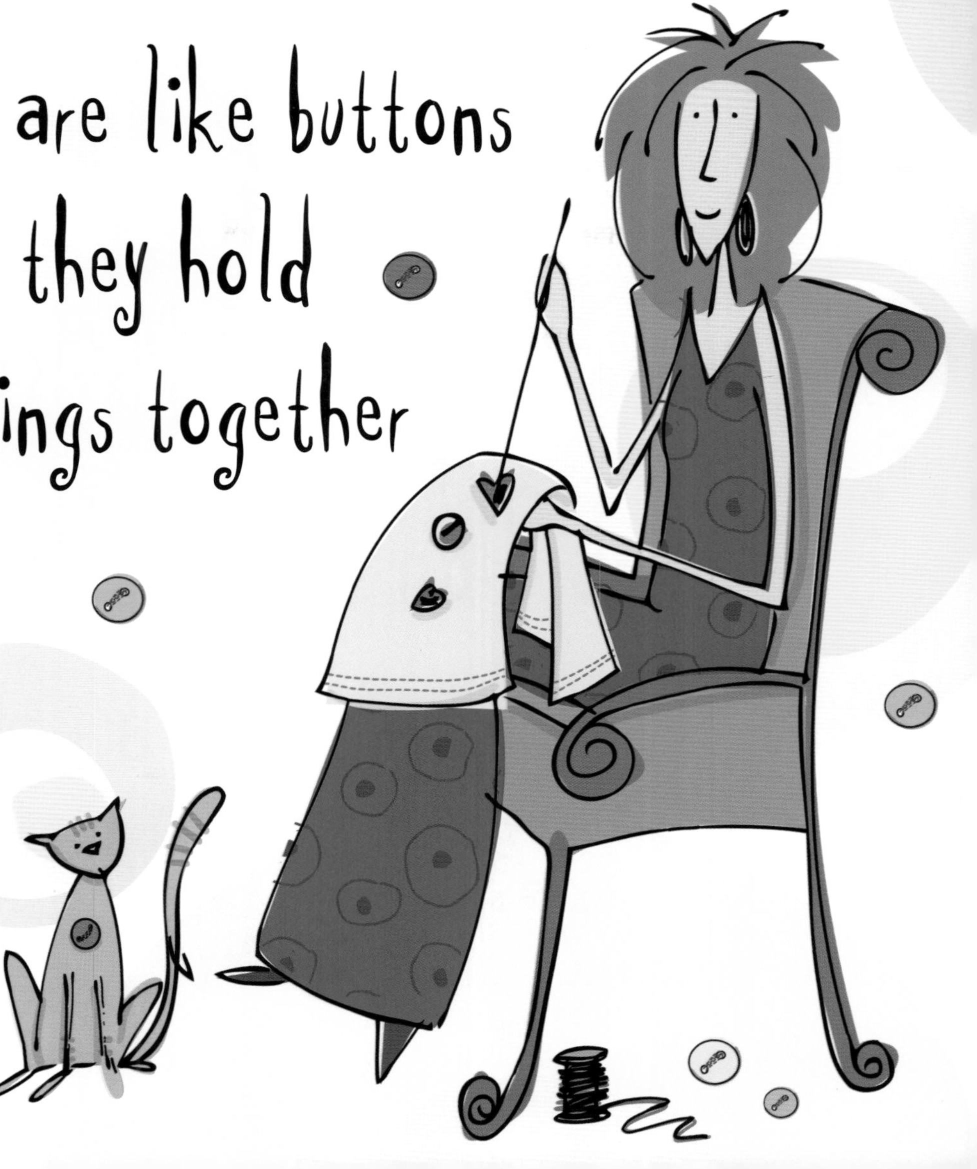

When I married Mr Right,
I didn't know his
first name was always

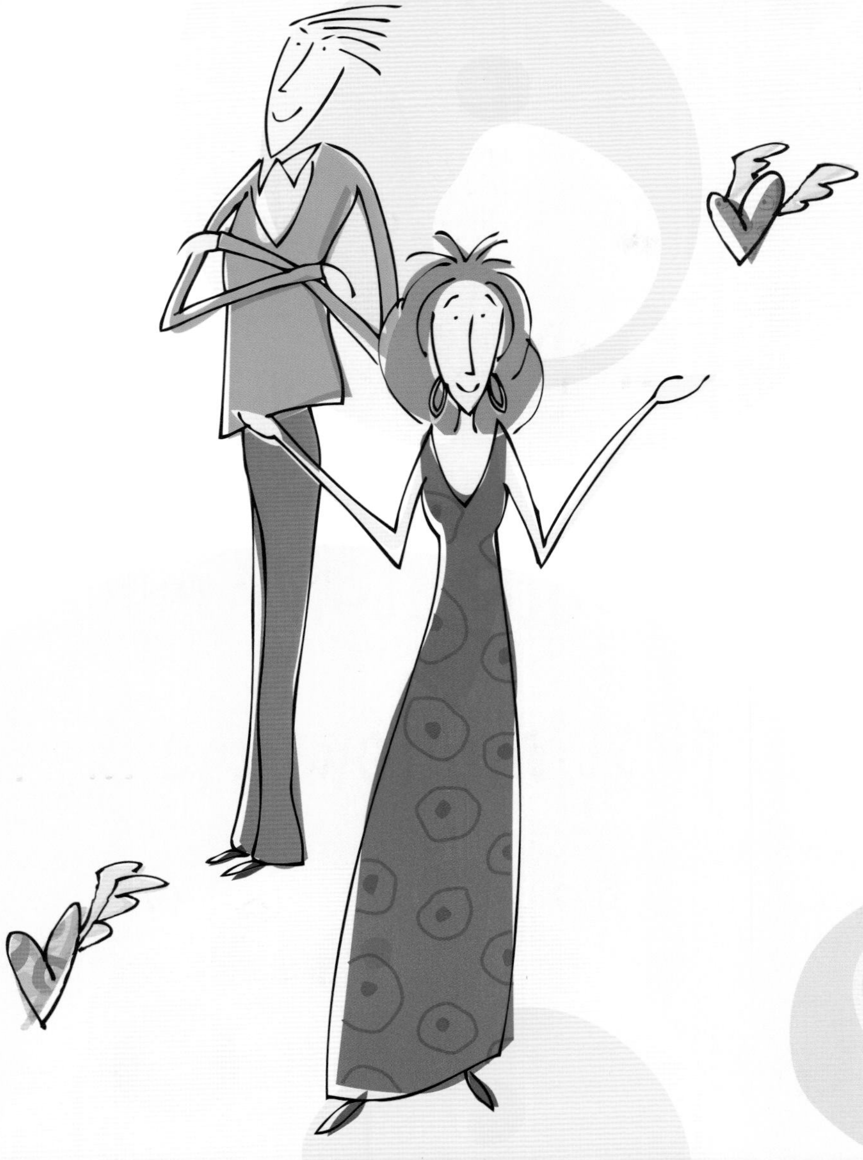

Don't try to
understand me
just love me

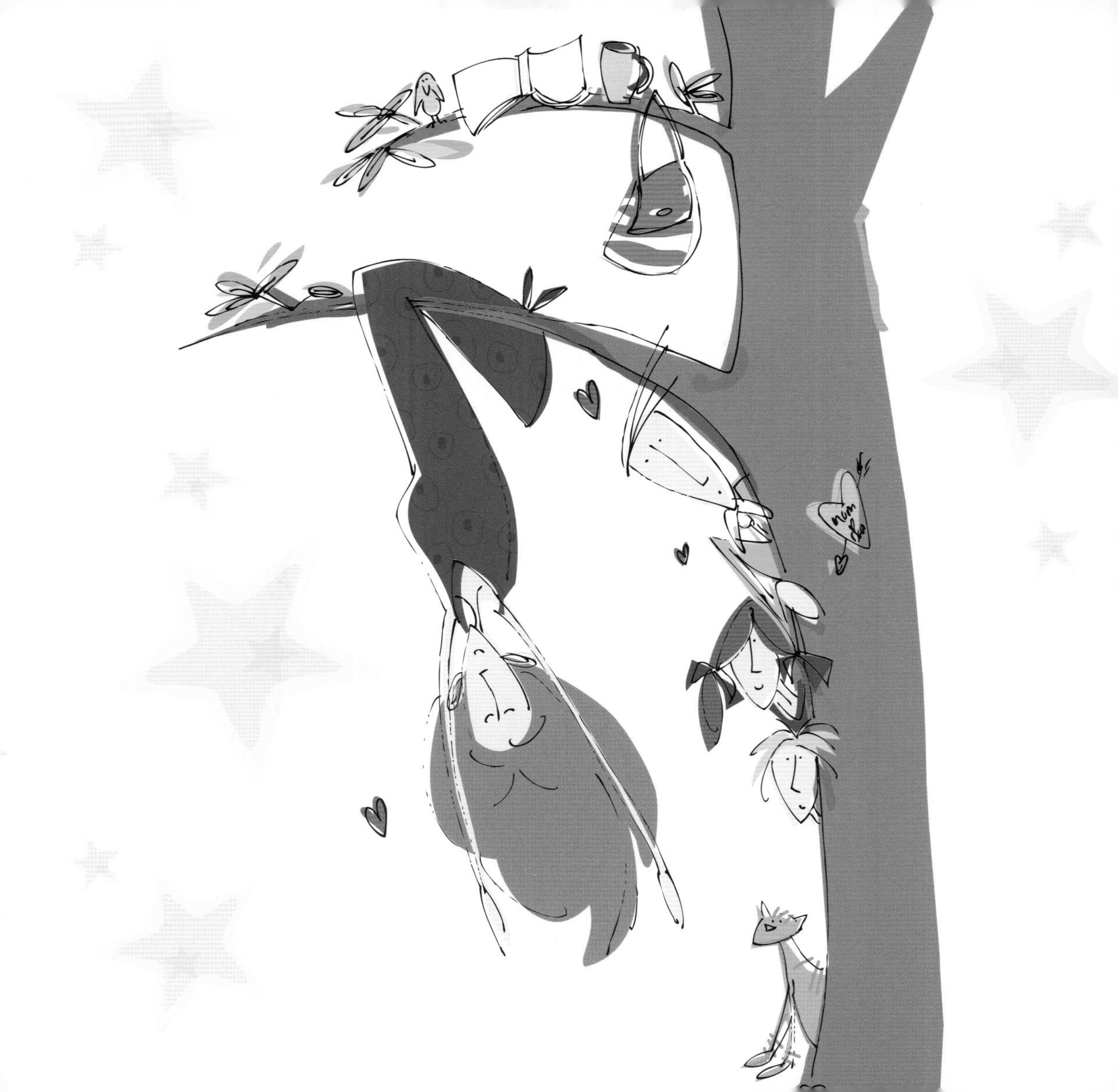
mum

Kids get colds,
men get flu
women get on with it

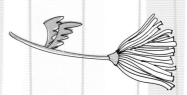

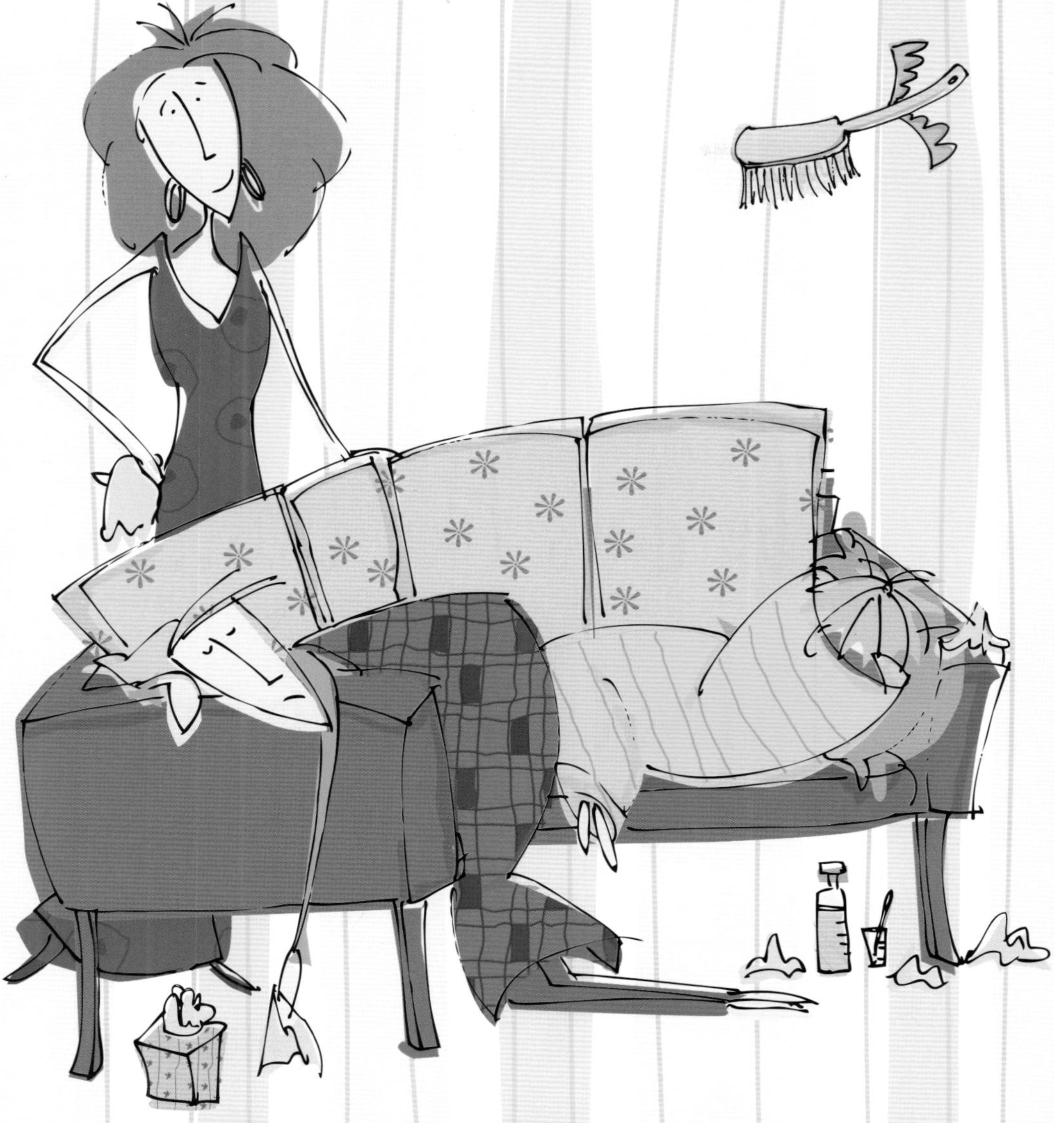

I knew there would be days like this...

...just not so many

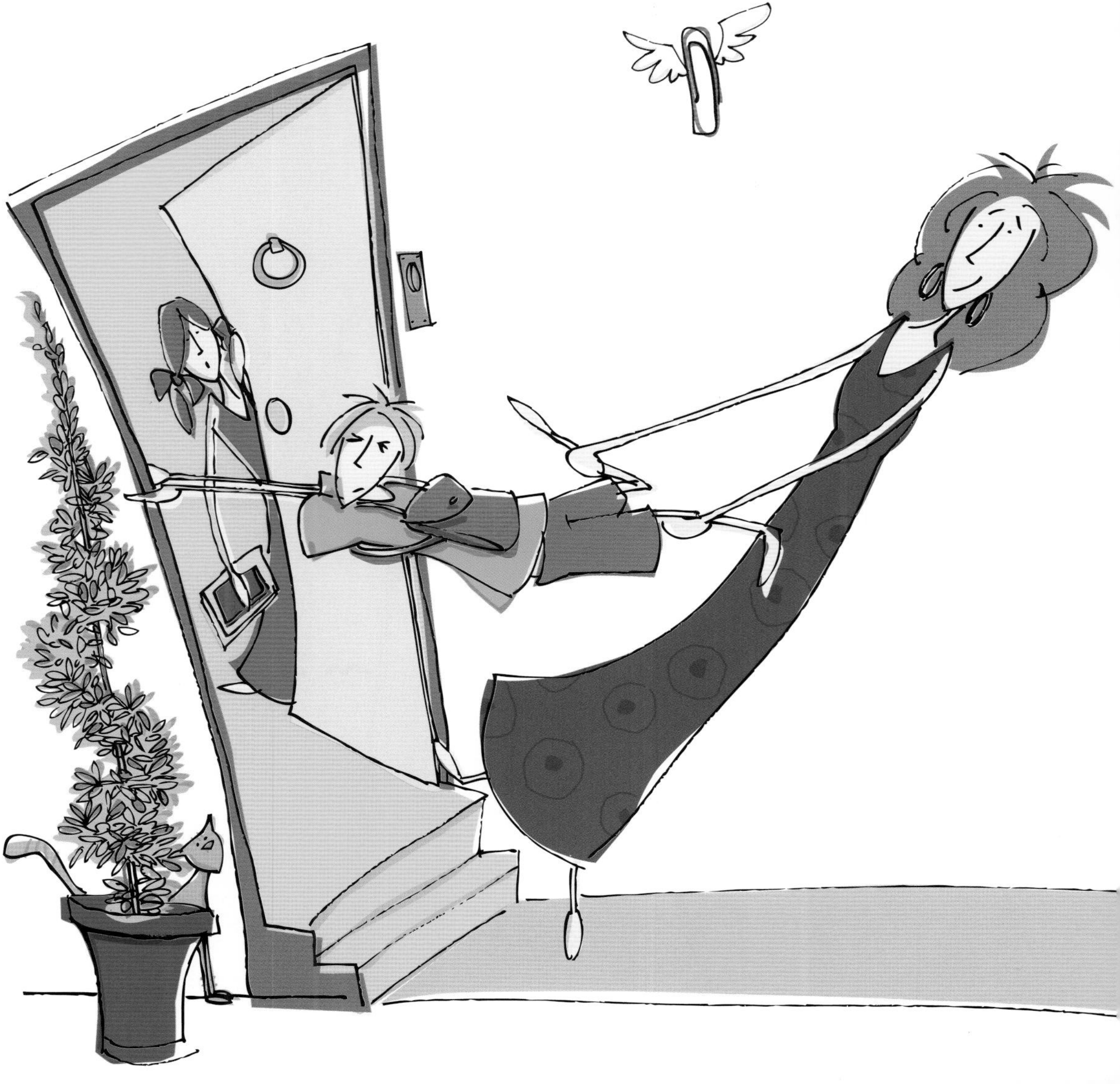

Born to be Wild

Seen it all,
done it all,
can't remember
most of it

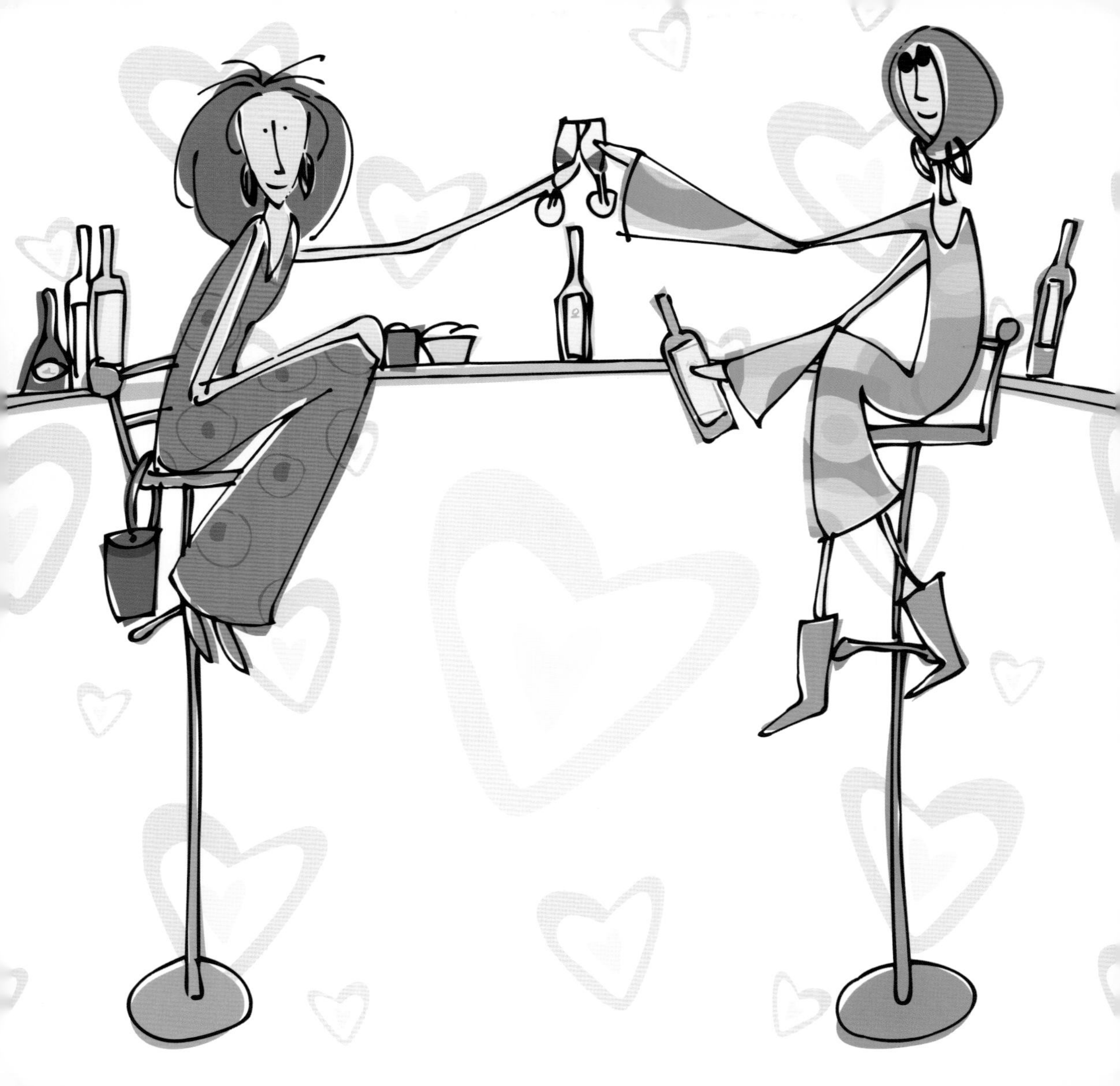

The whole world
is about three
drinks behind

I'm on a Gin and Tonic diet, so far I've lost two days

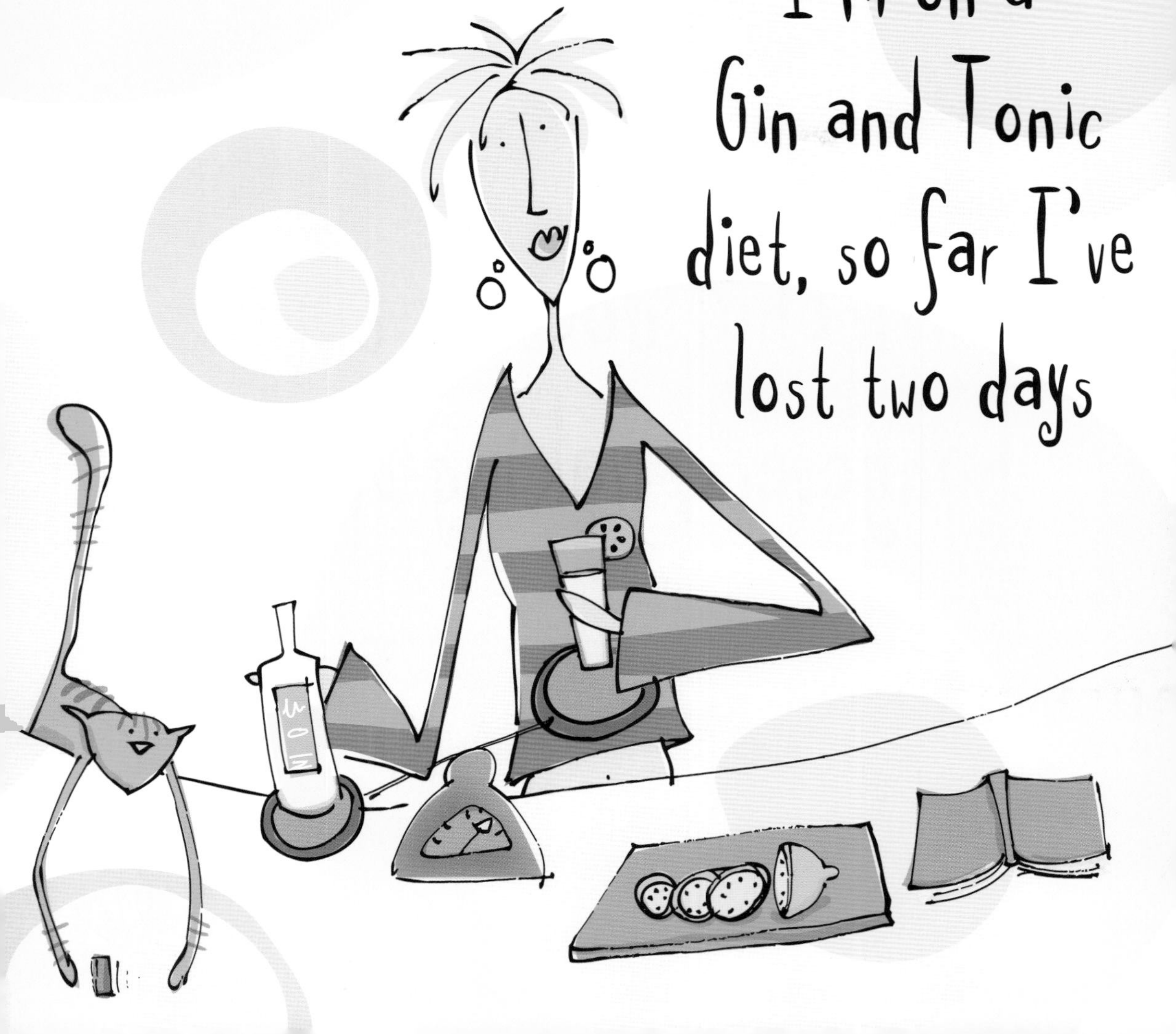

Alcohol doesn't cause hangovers, waking up does

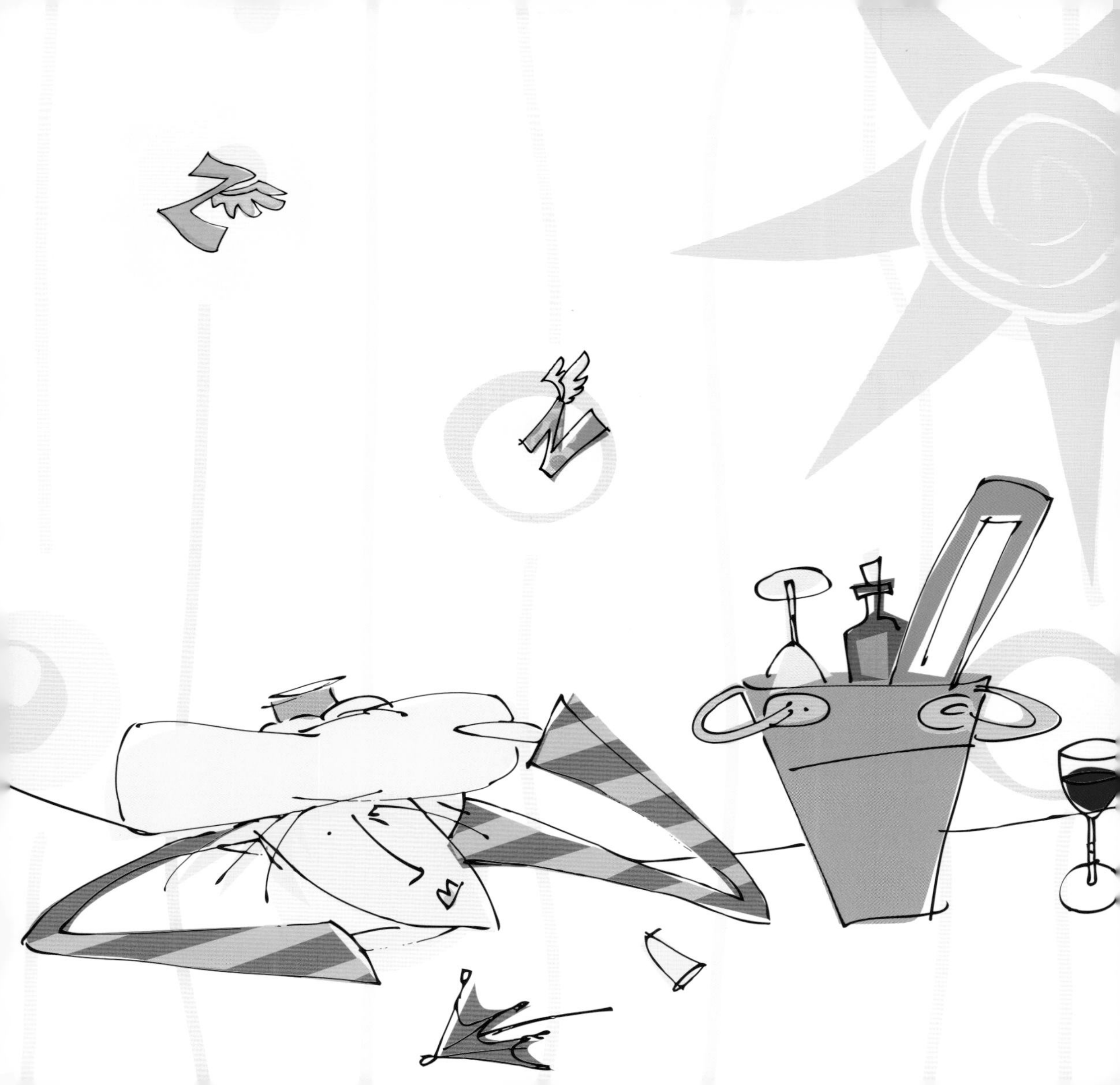

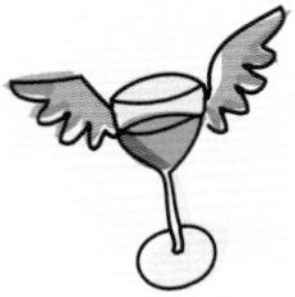

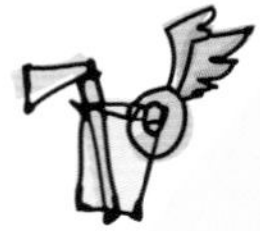

If you obey all the rules
you miss all the fun

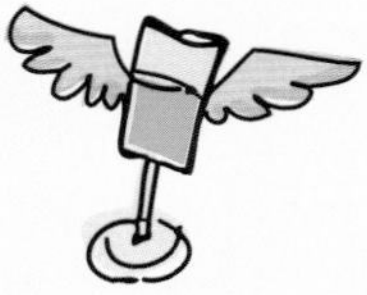

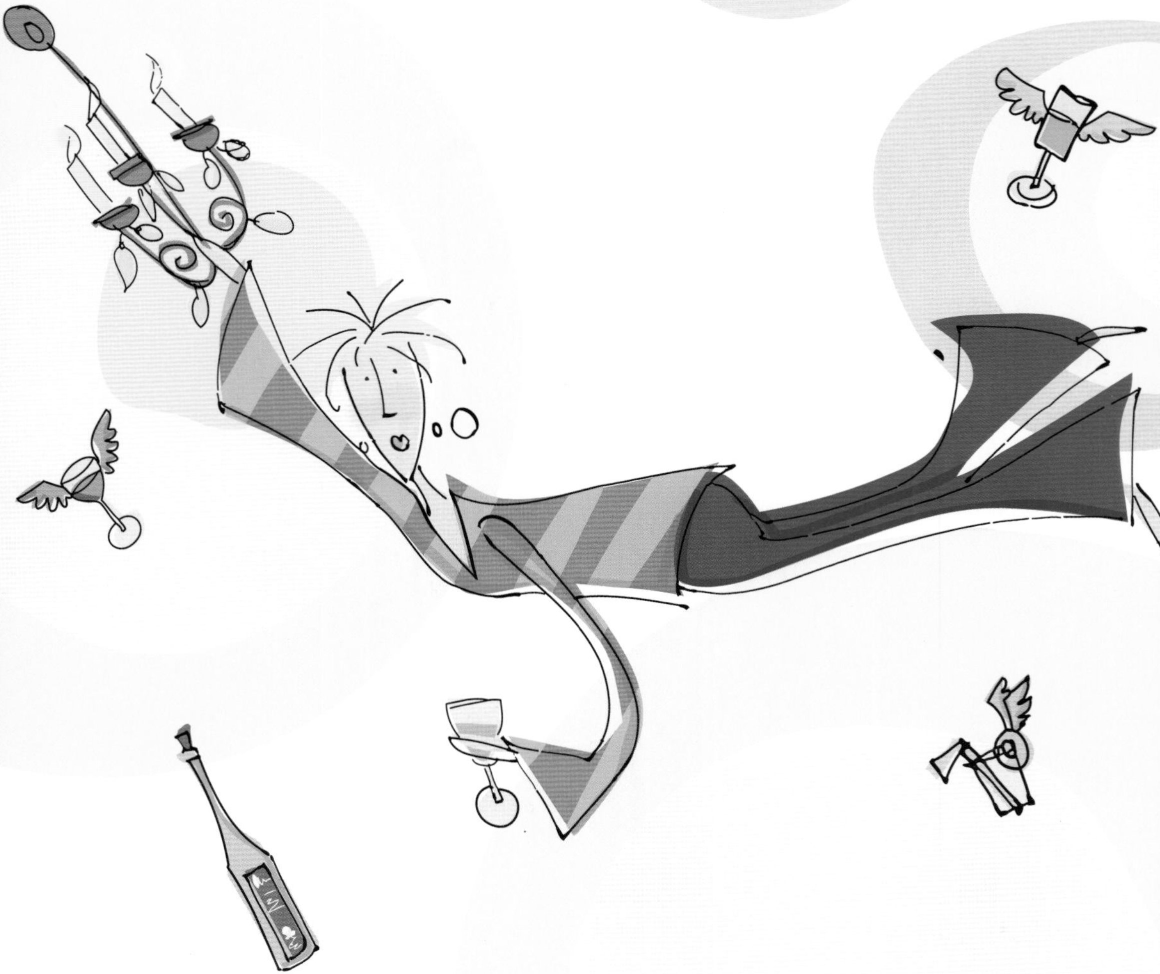

One Tequila,
two Tequila,
three Tequila,
floor!

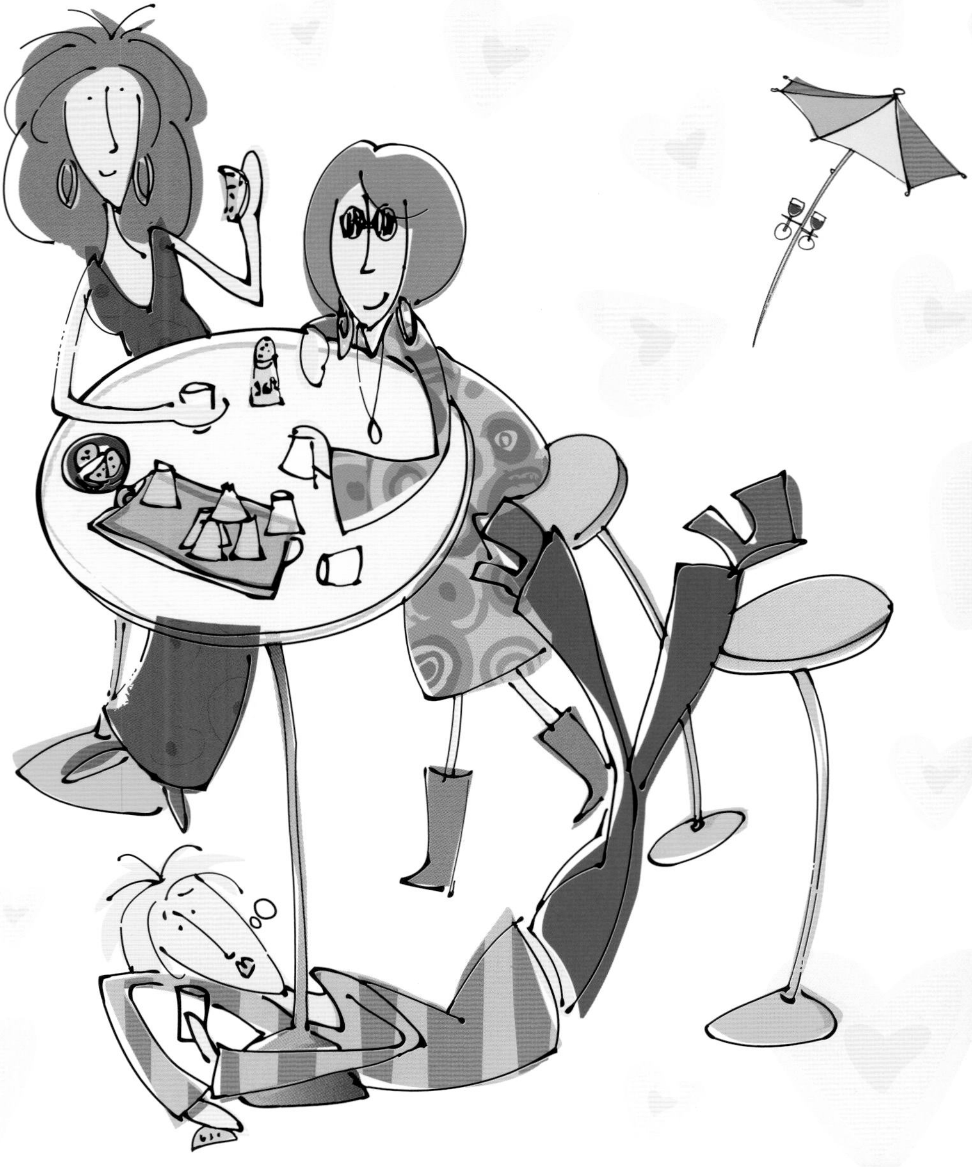

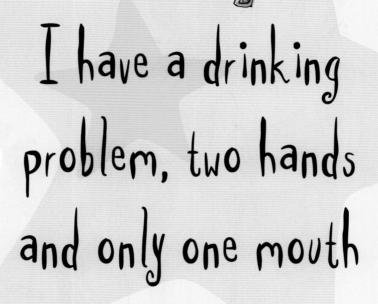

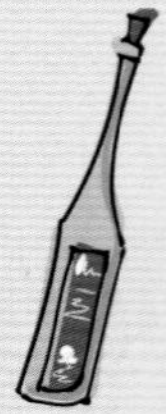

I have a drinking
problem, two hands
and only one mouth

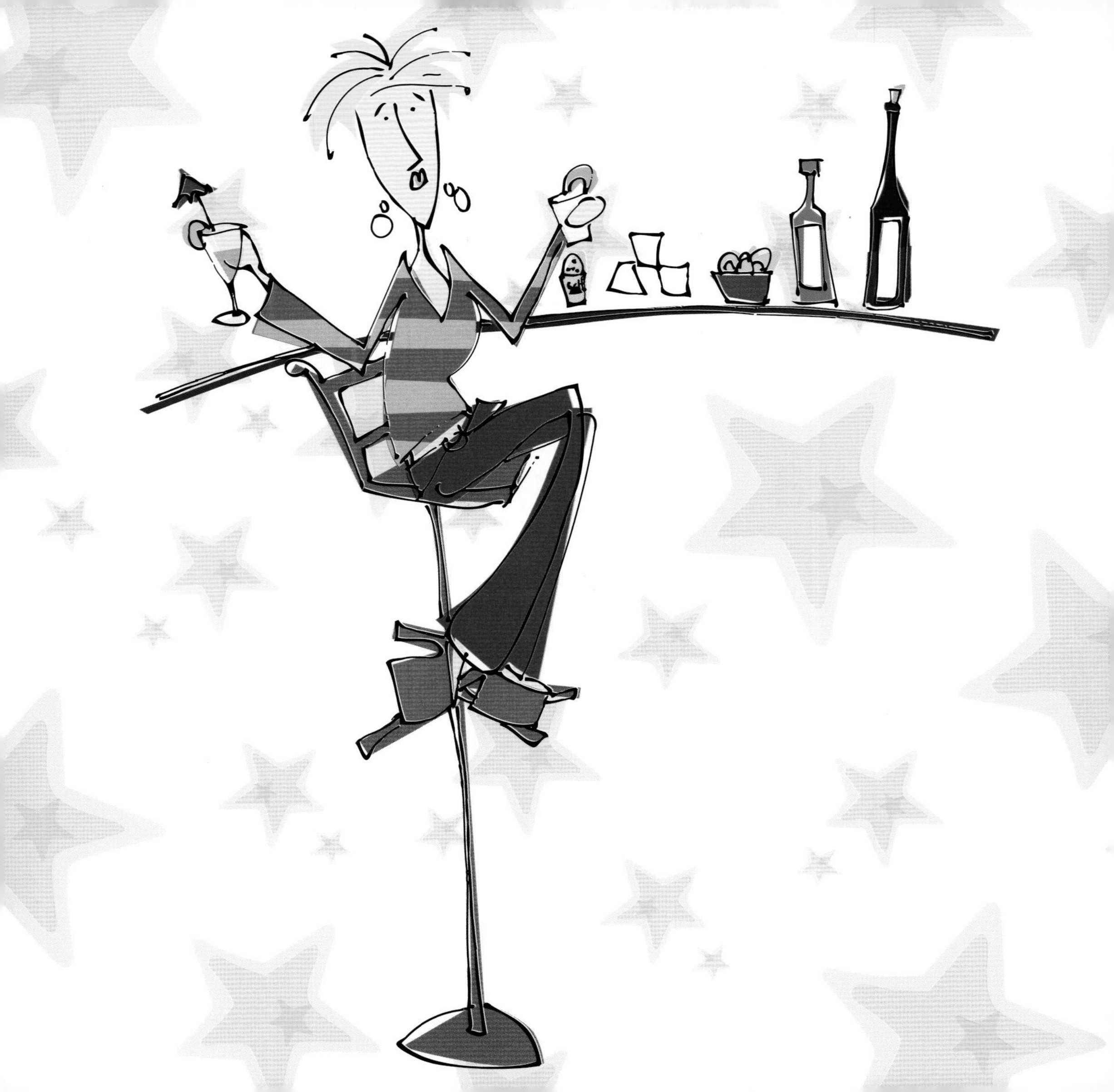

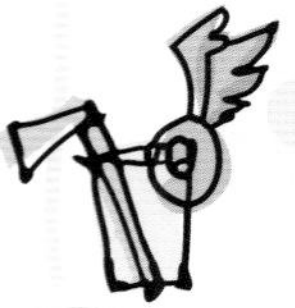

I take life with
a pinch of salt,
a wedge of lime
and a shot of tequila

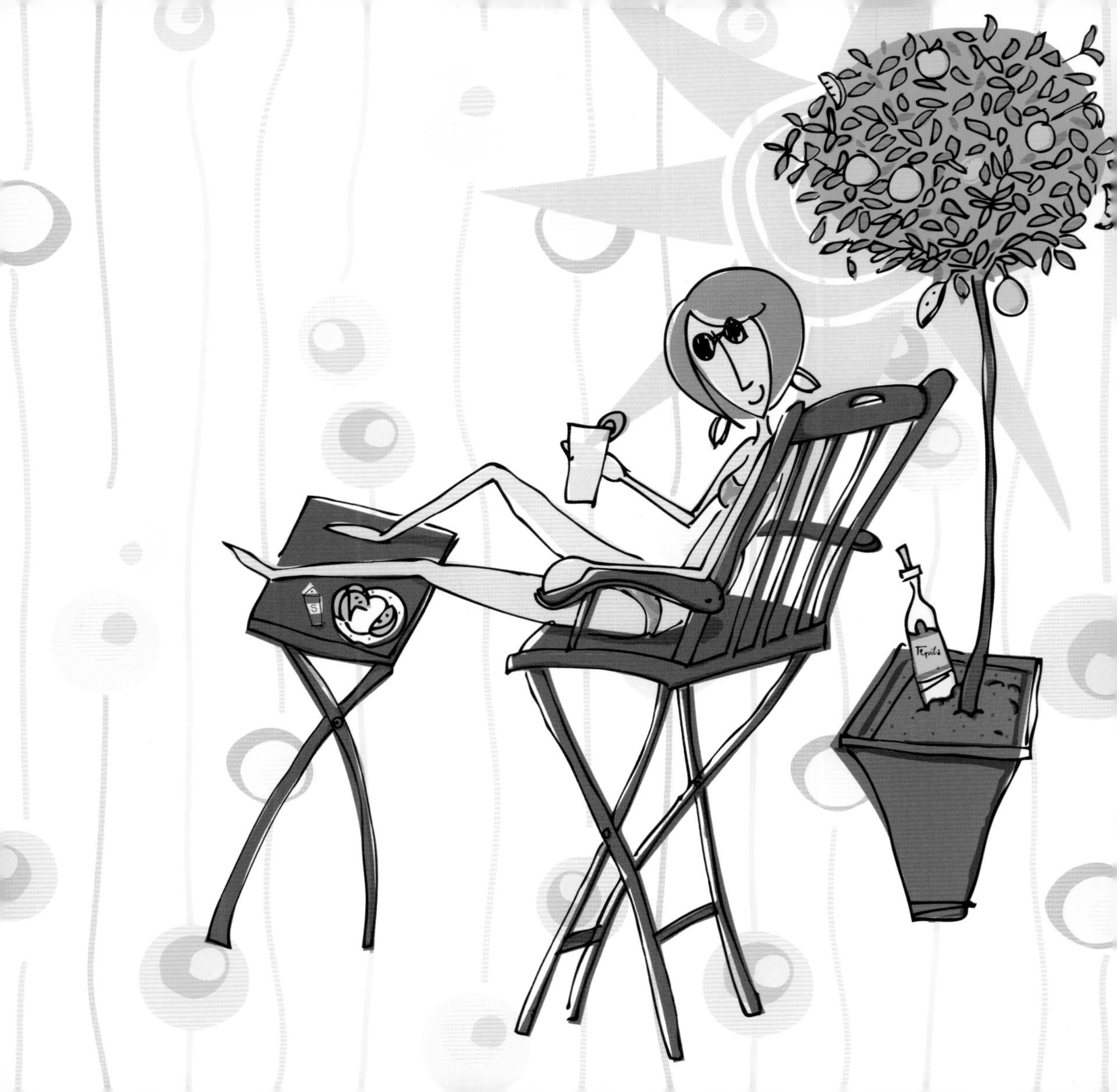
S
Tequila

Born to be a
Domestic Goddess

Housework won't kill you but why take the chance?

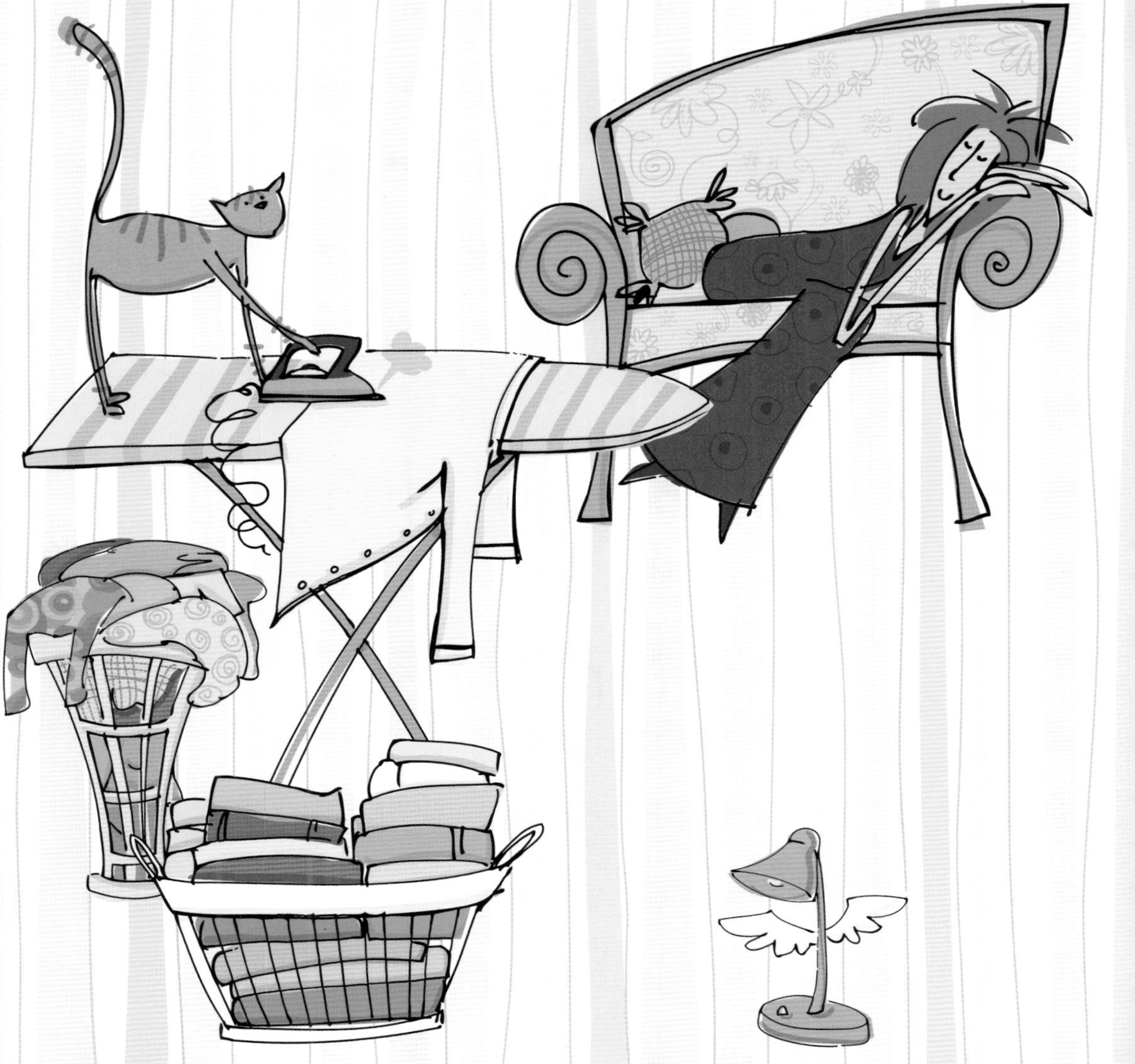

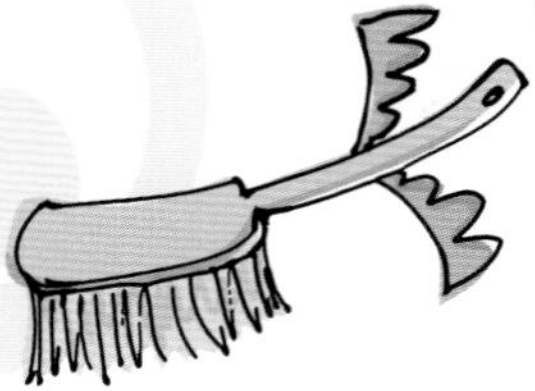

This is a self cleaning kitchen, so clean up after yourself

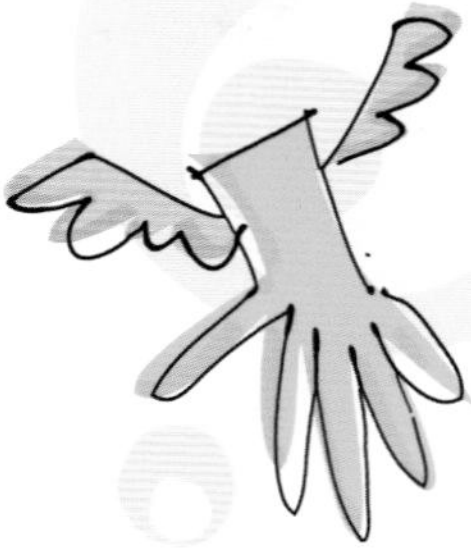

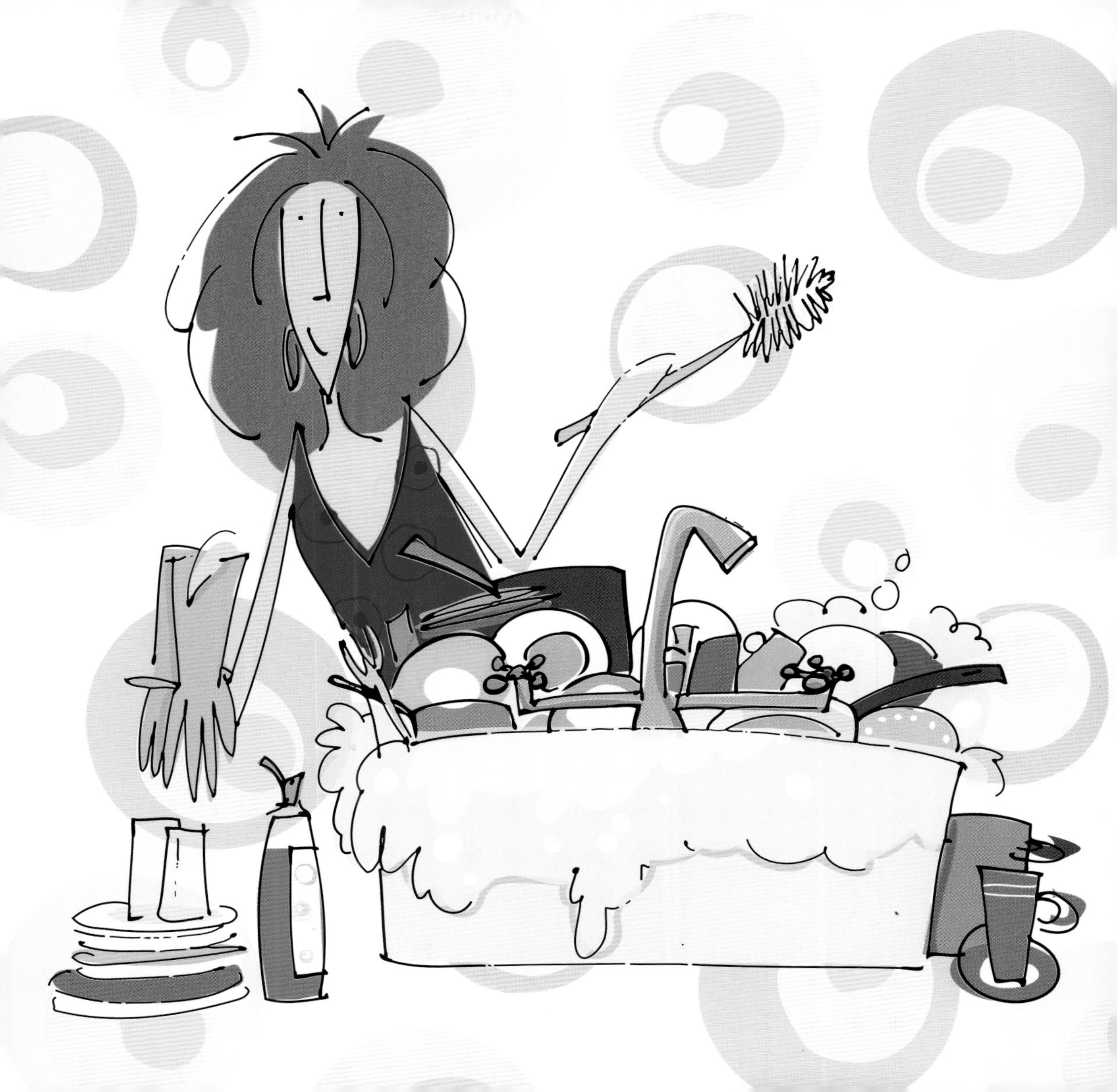

You can touch the dust,
but please don't write in it

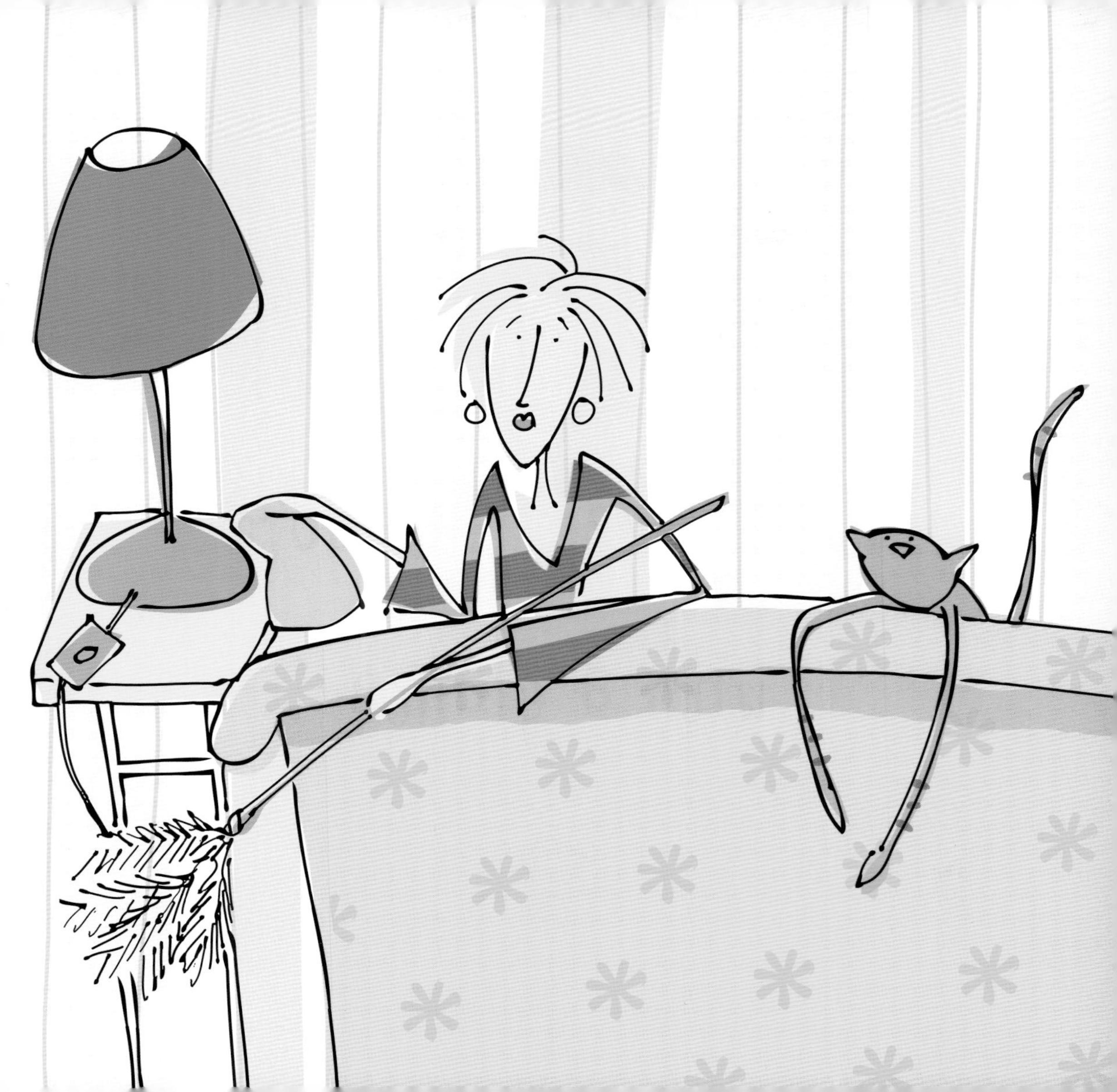

My idea of housework
is to sweep the room
with a glance

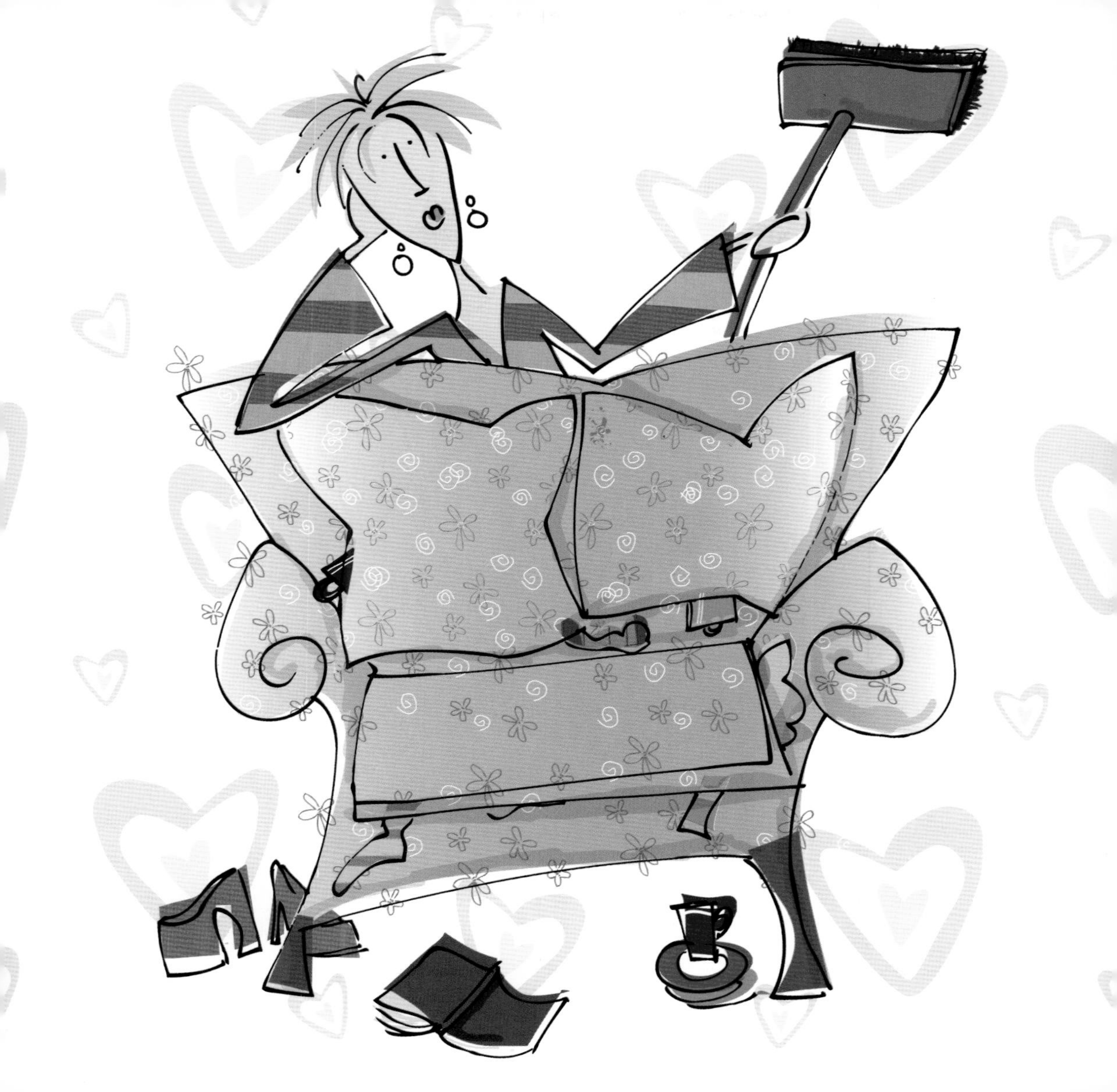

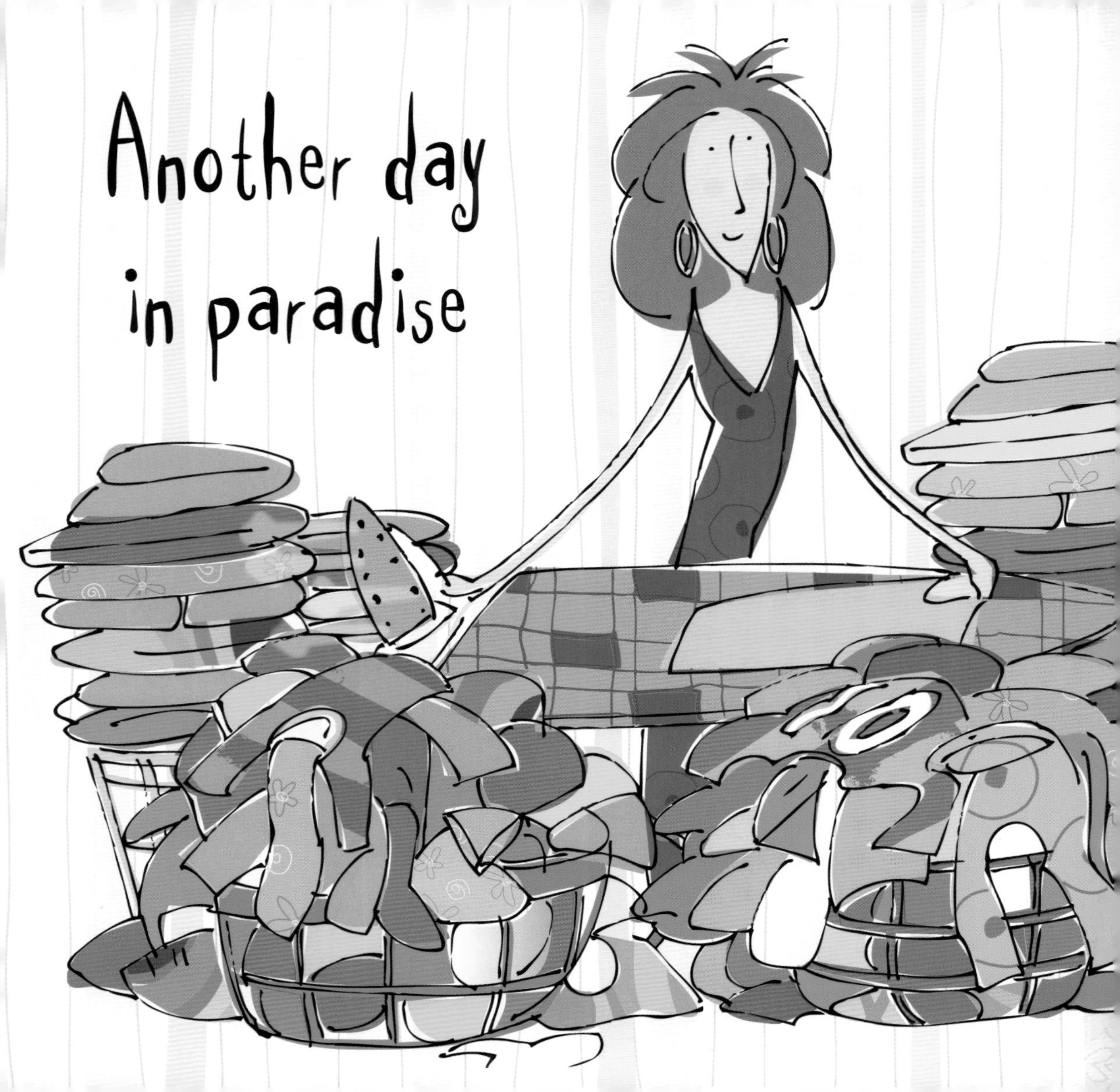
Another day
in paradise

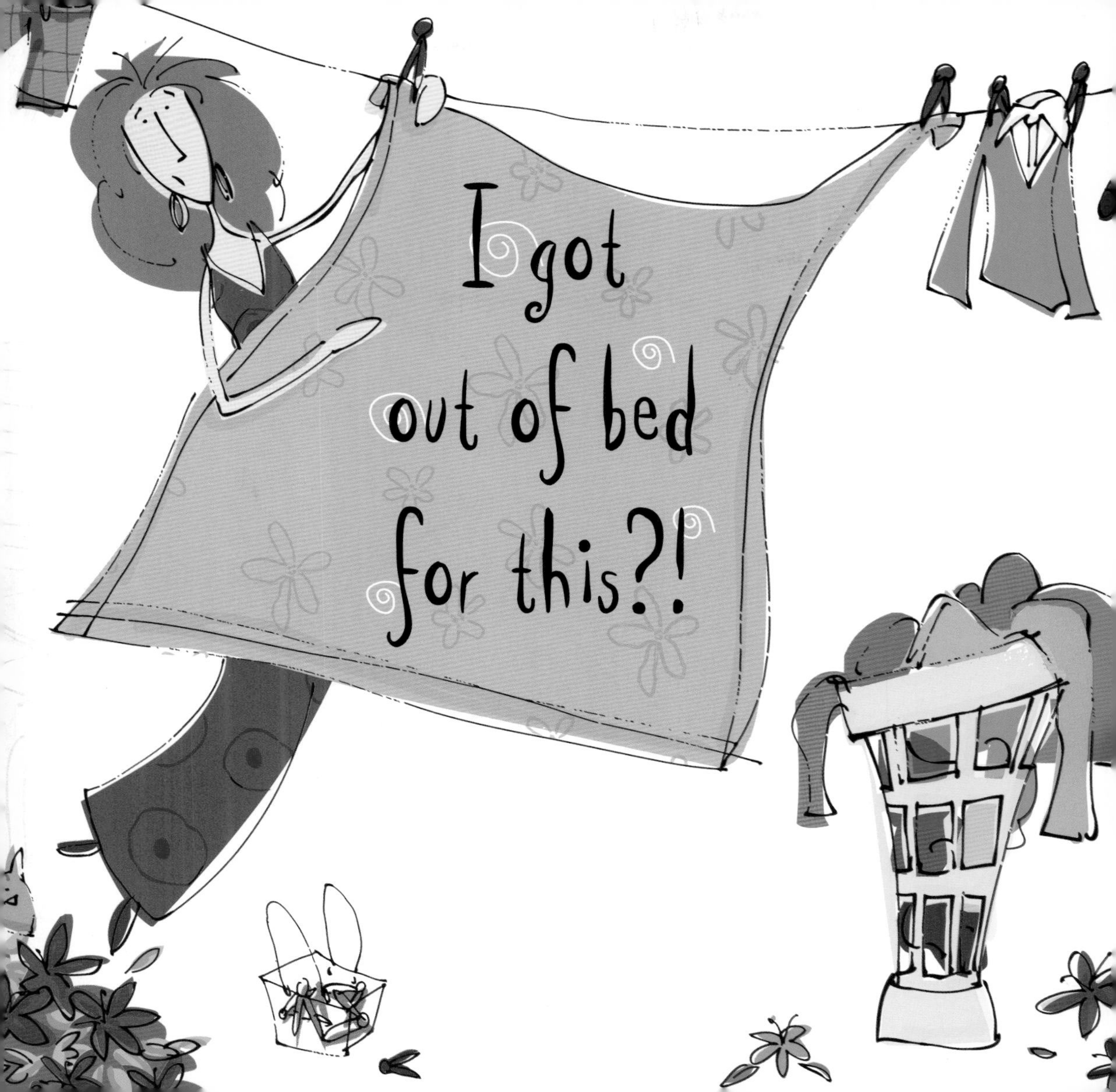
I got
out of bed
for this?!

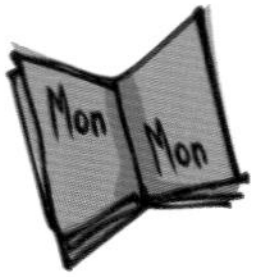
Mon
Mon

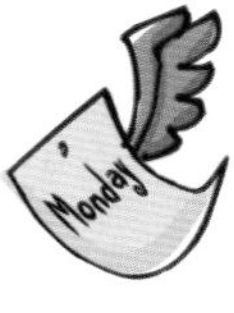
Monday

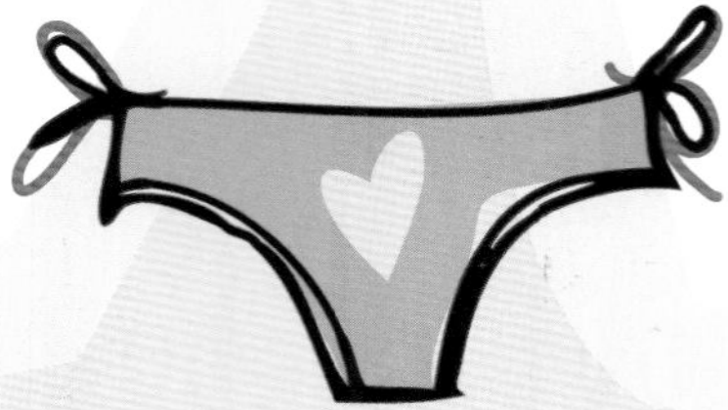

It's been Monday
all week

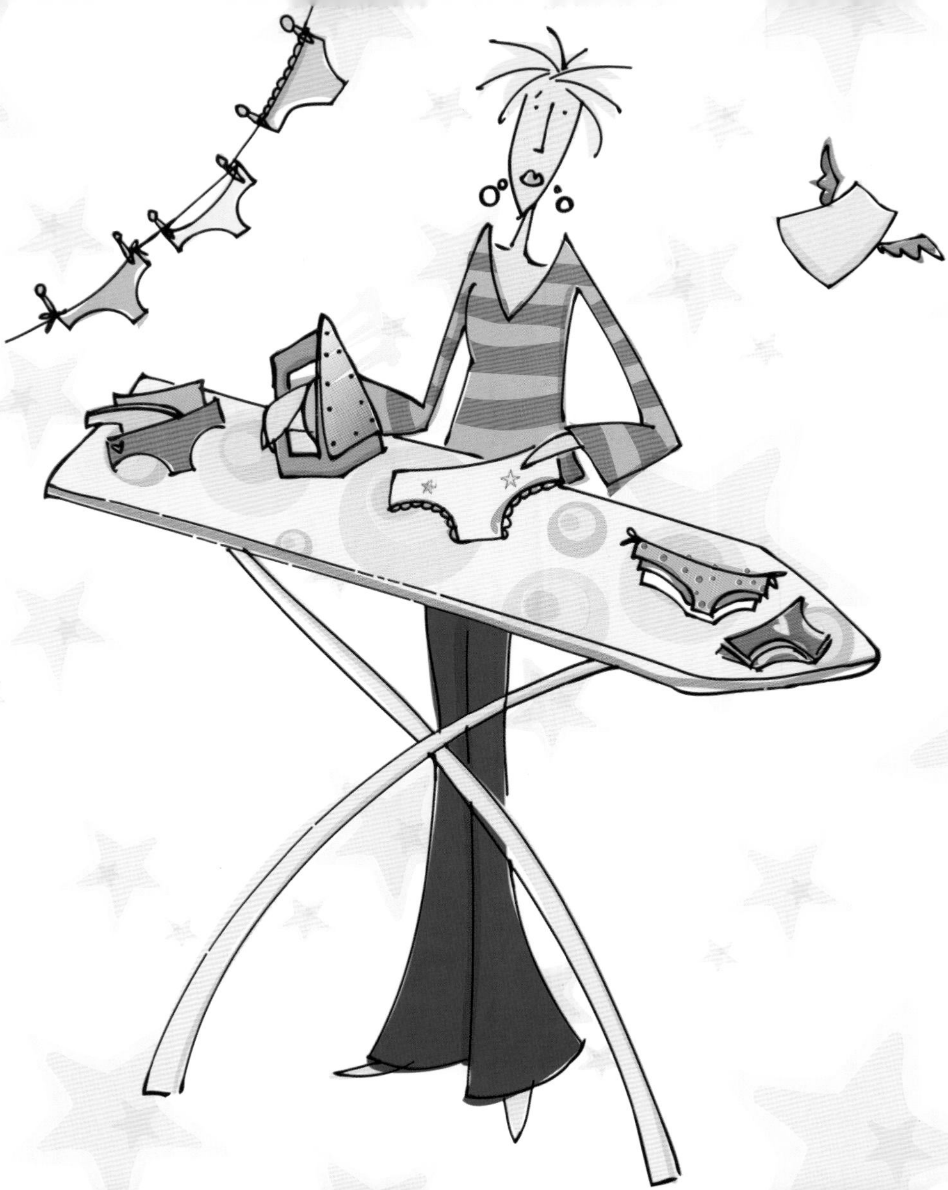

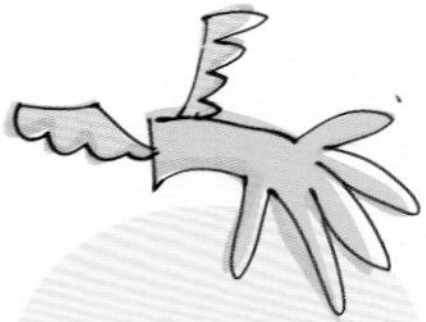

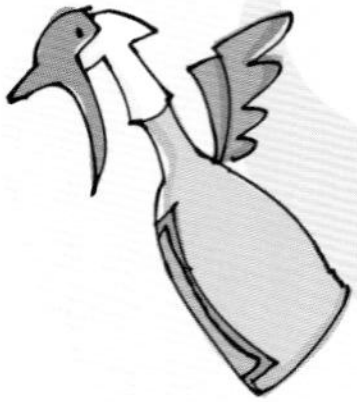

Instead of cleaning
the house I just
turn off the lights

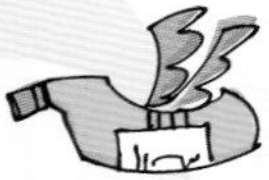

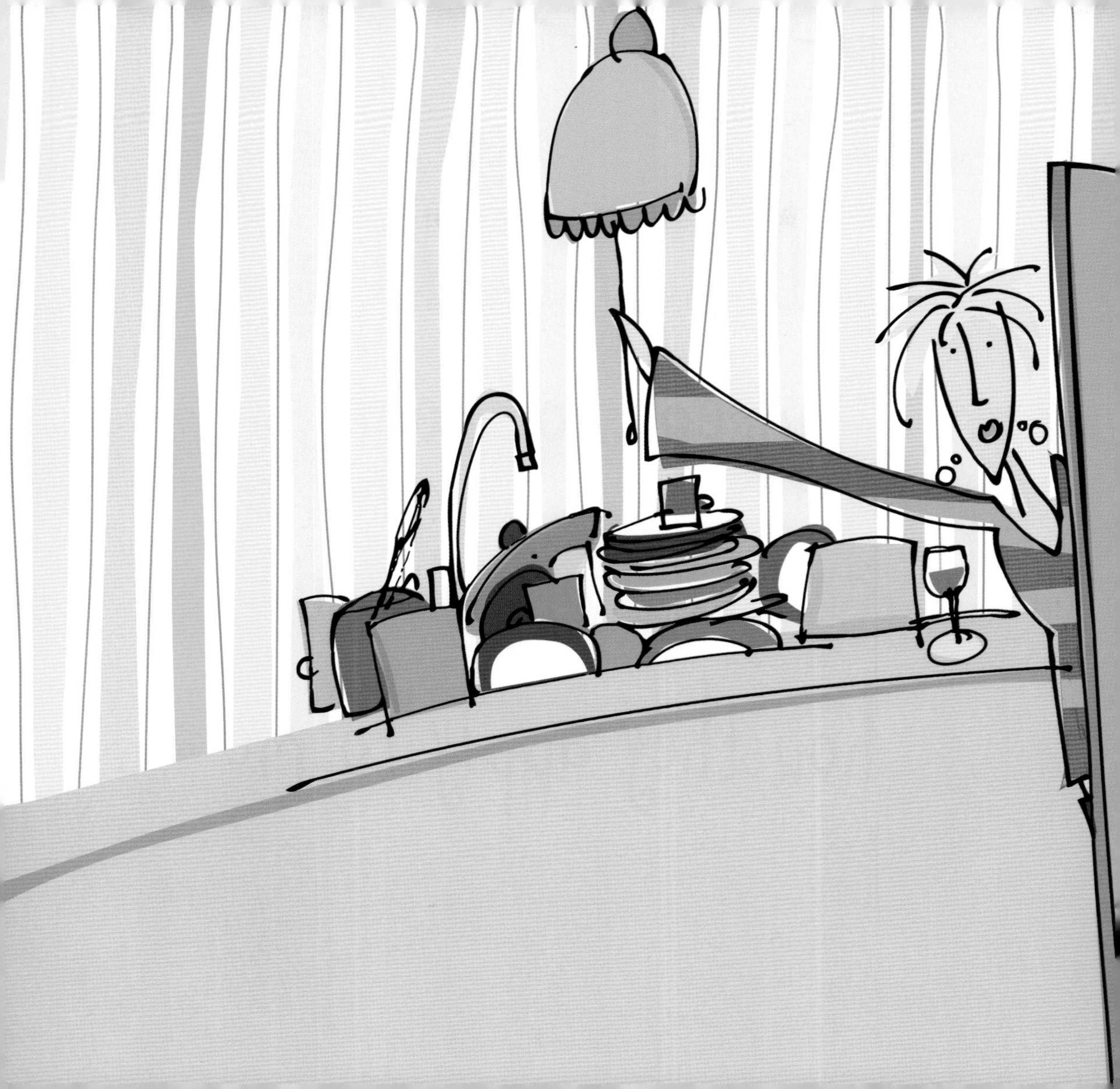

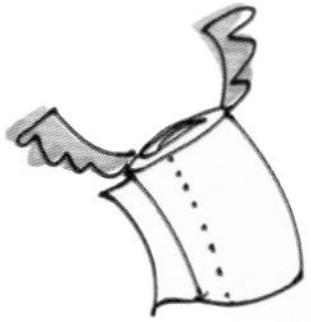

I understand the concepts of cooking and cleaning just not how they apply to me

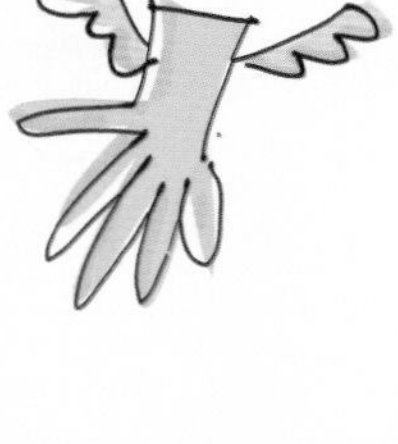

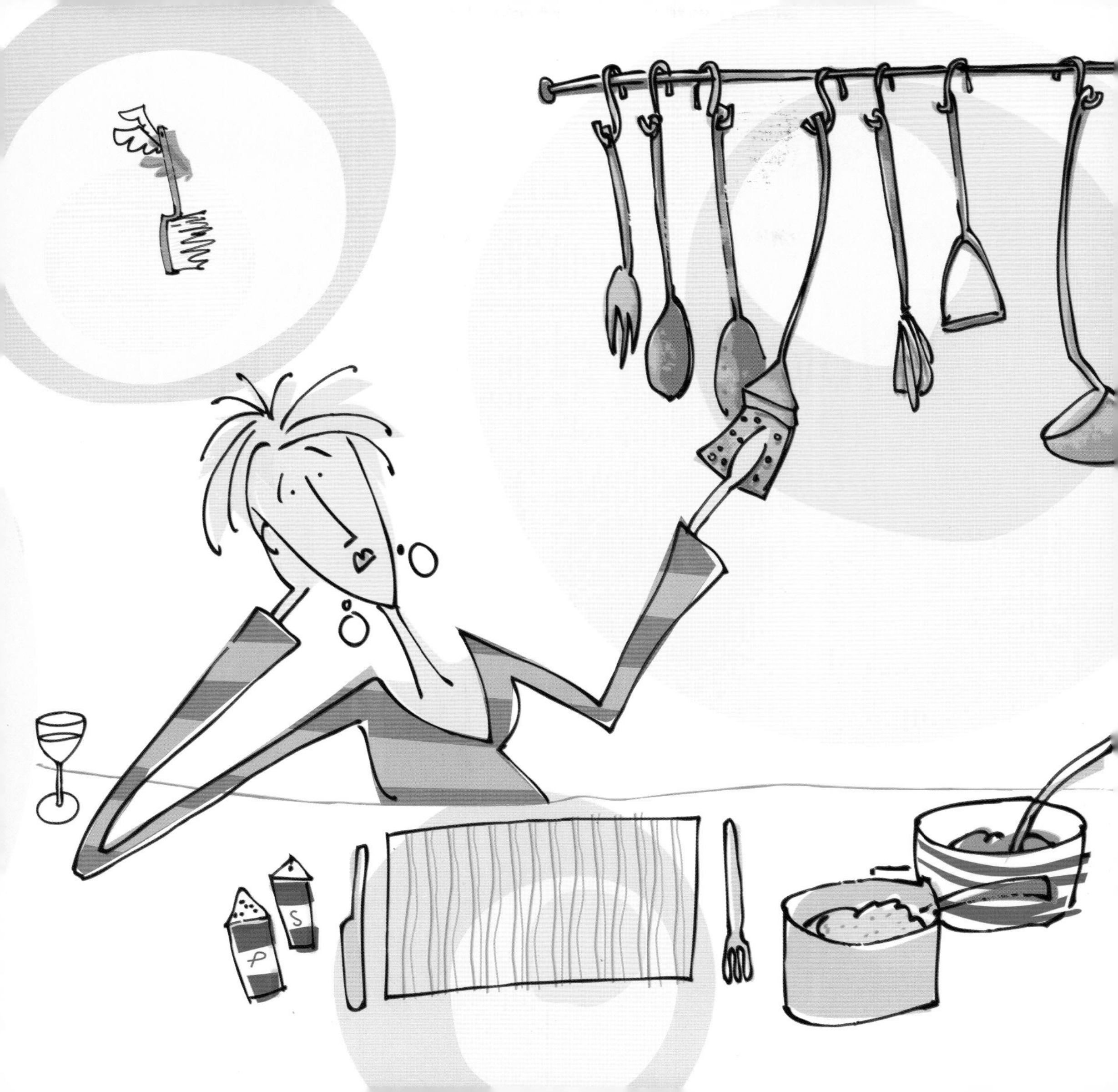
S
P

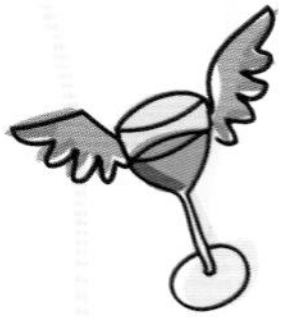 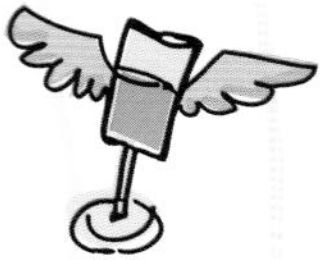

I love to cook with wine,
sometimes I even put
it in the food

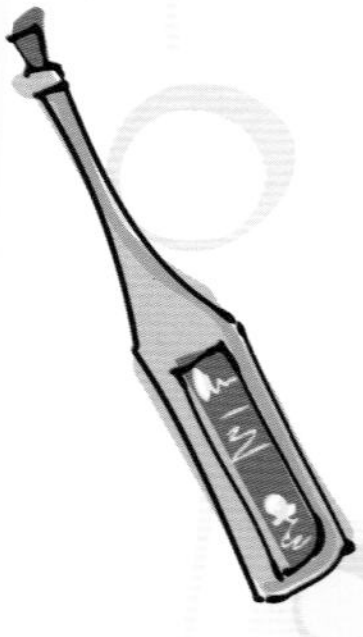

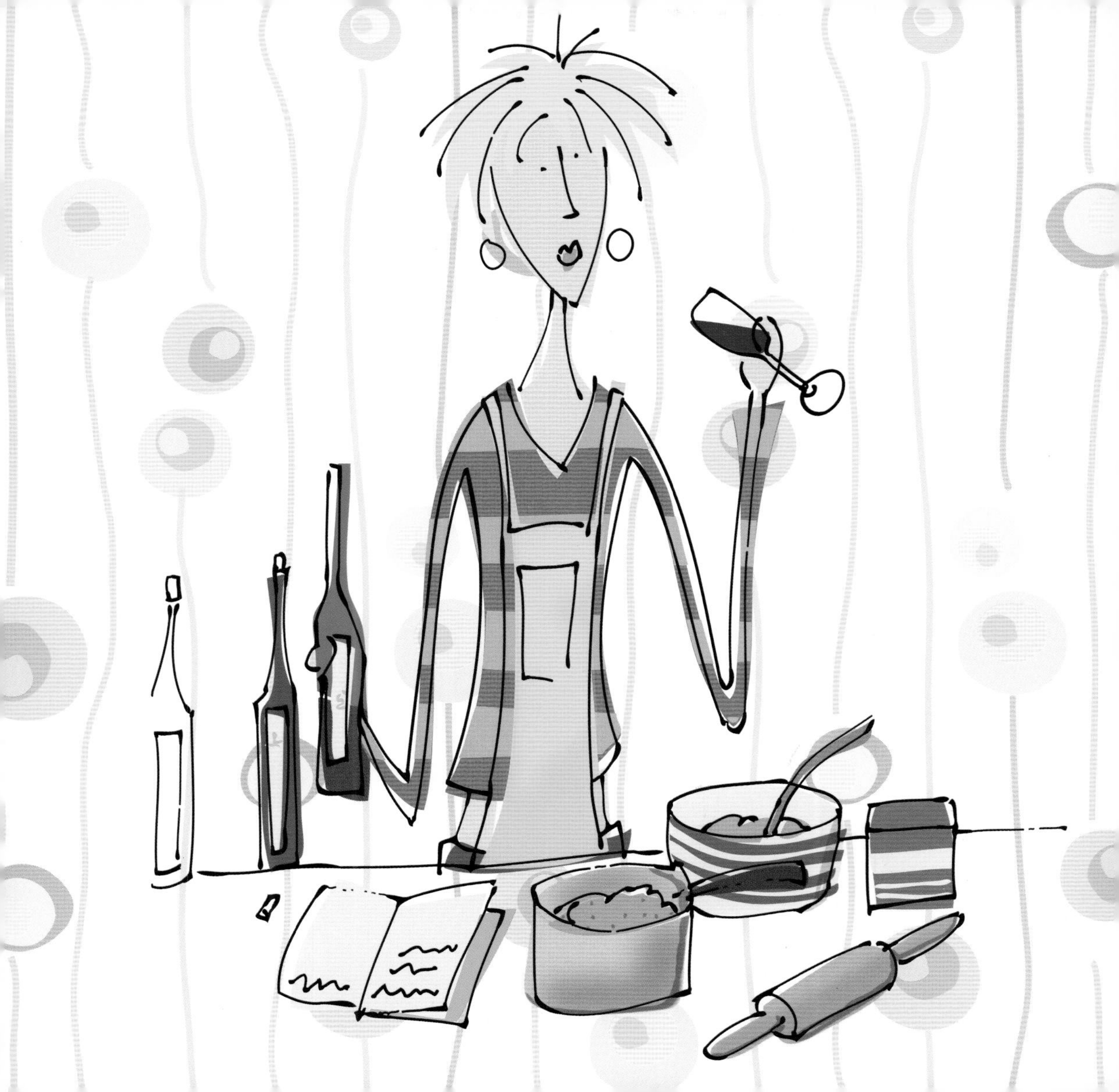

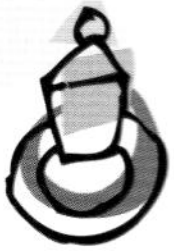

If you don't
like my cooking
lower your standards

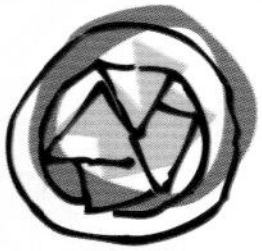

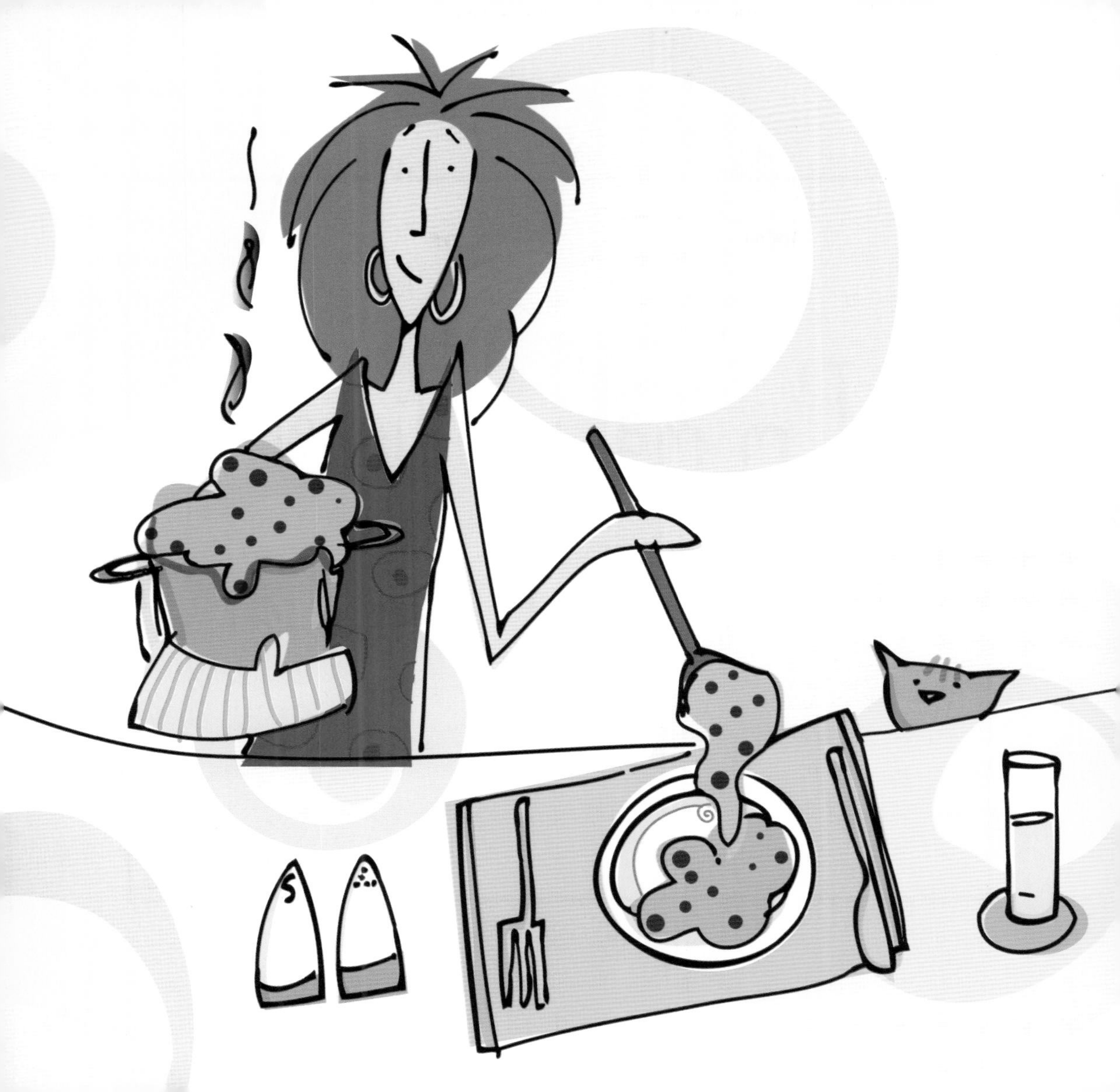
S

I'm making dinner
as fast as I can dial

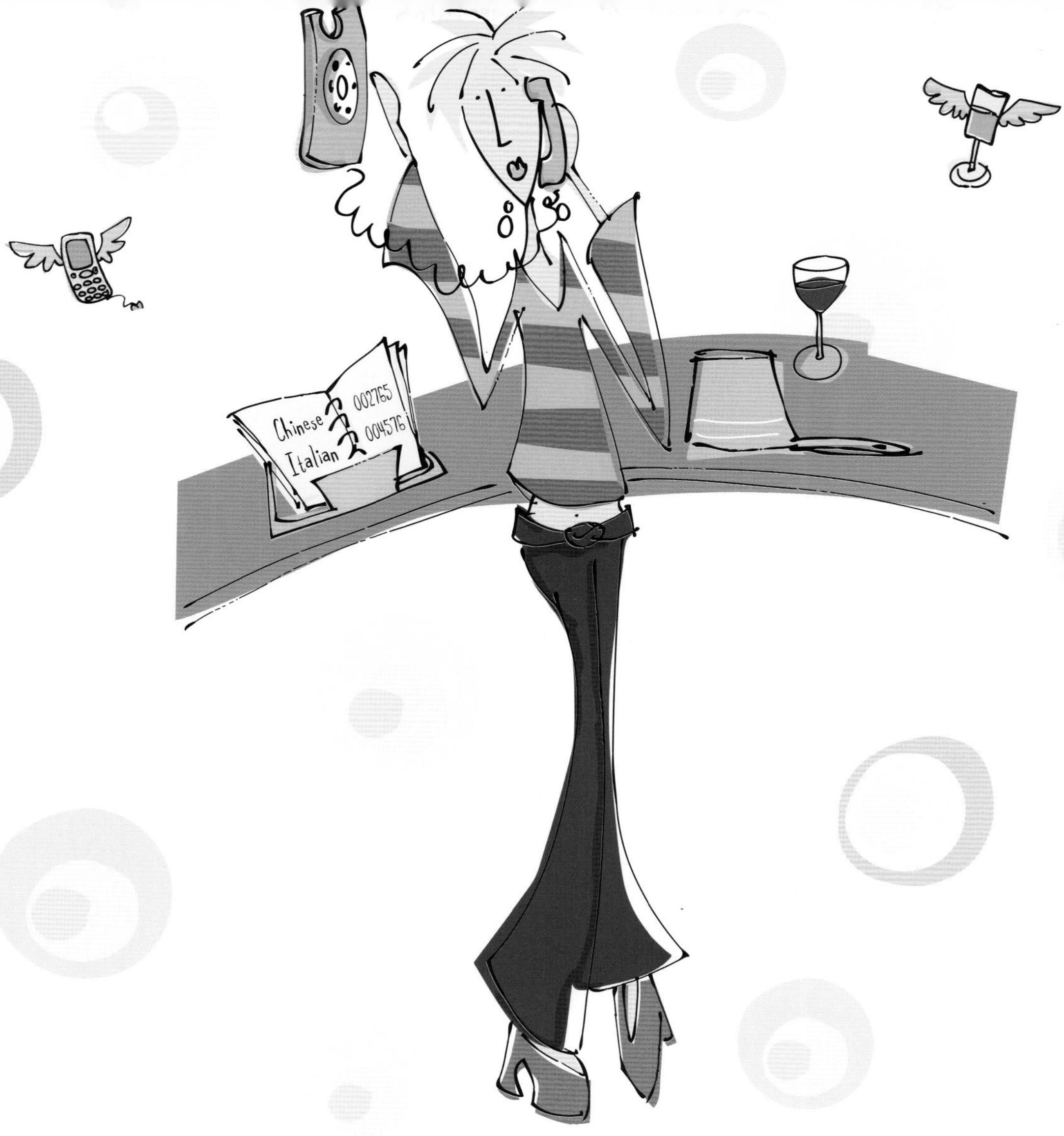
Chinese 002765
Italian 004576

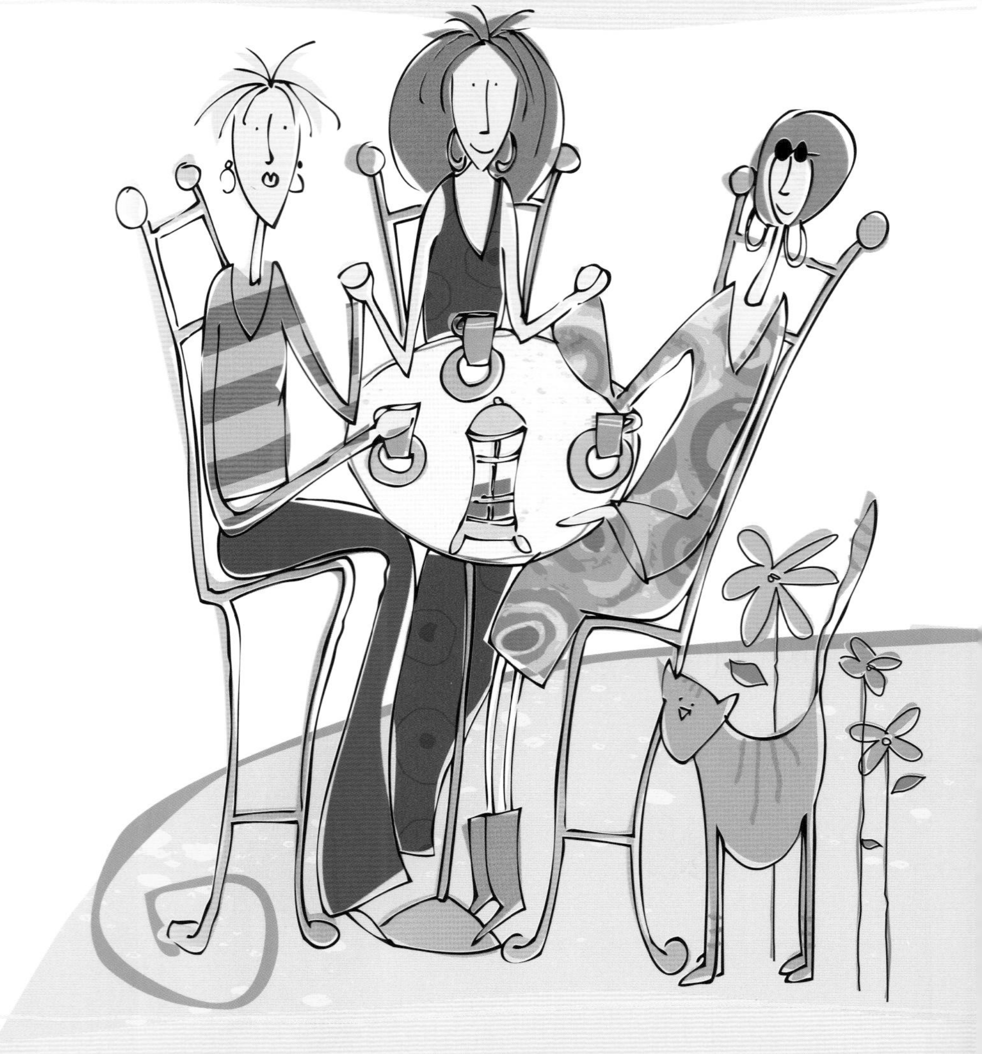

Born to be Friends

When friends meet,
hearts warm

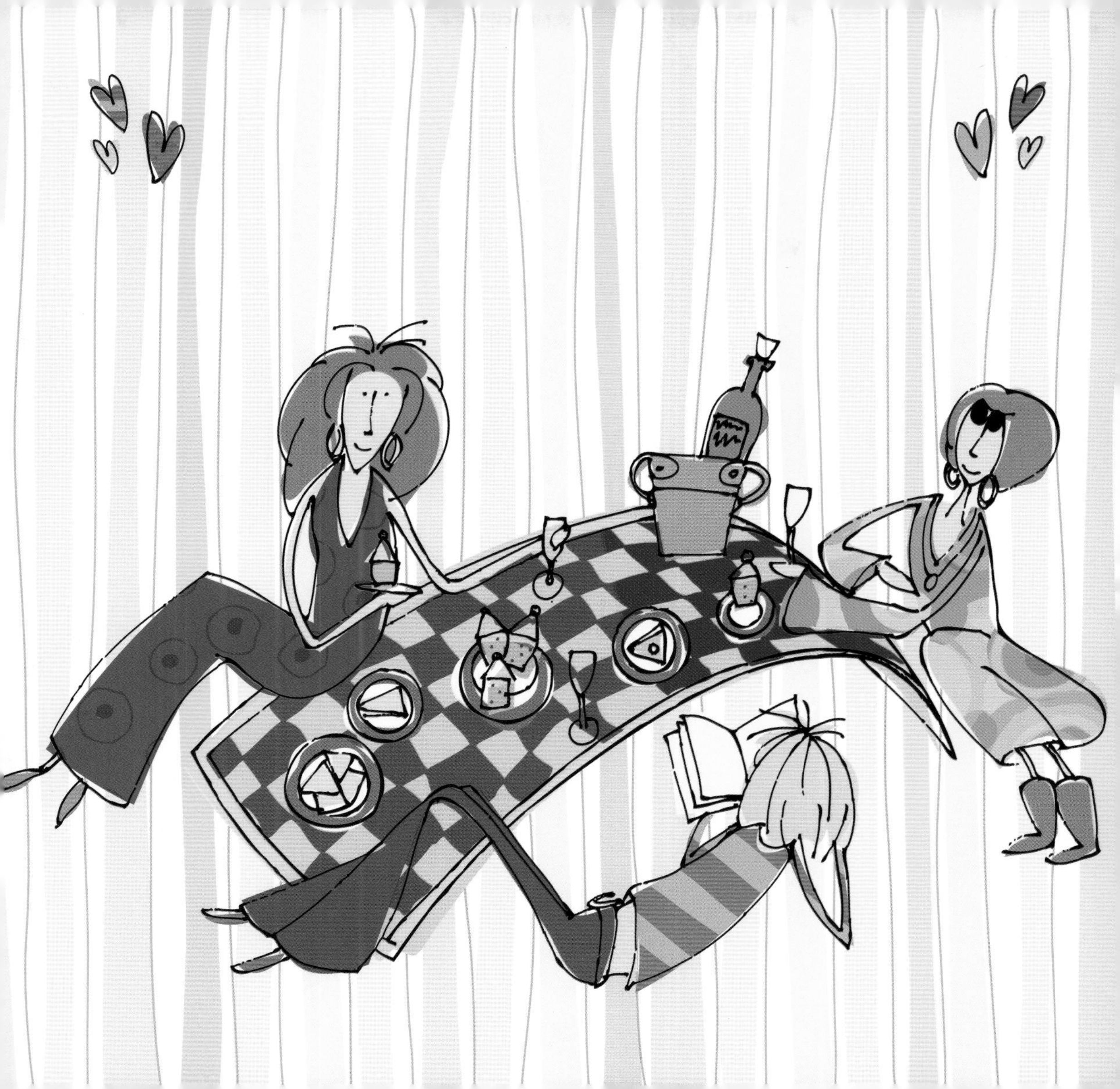

You'll always be my friend,
you know too much

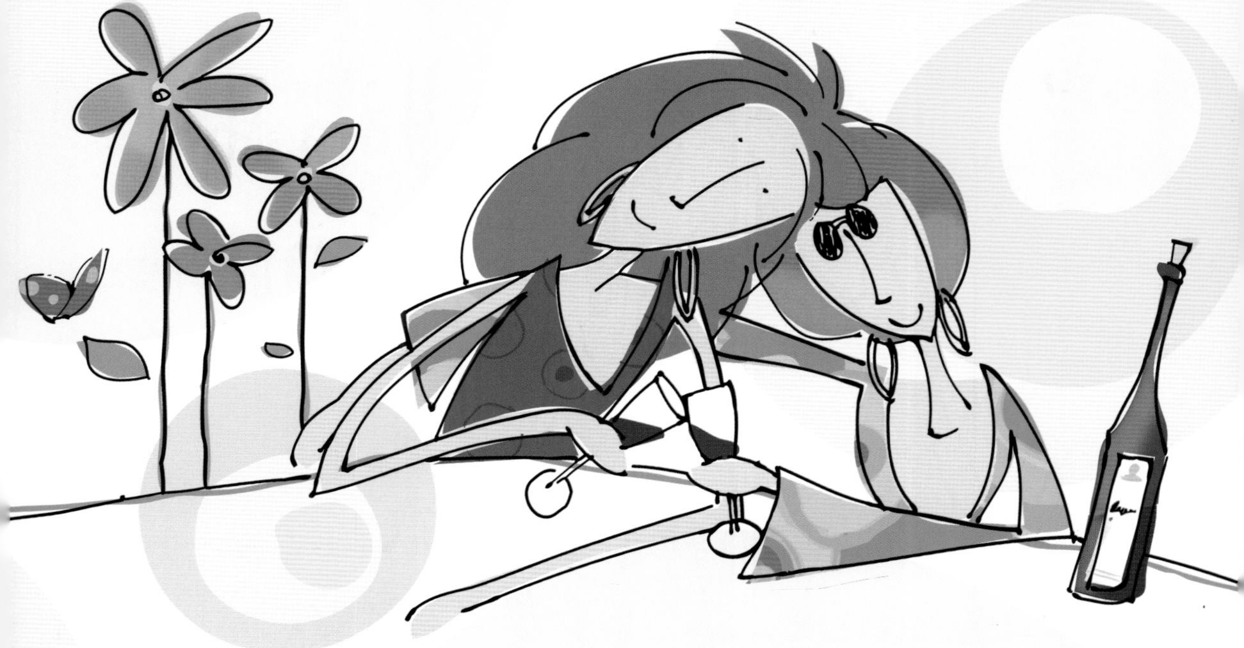

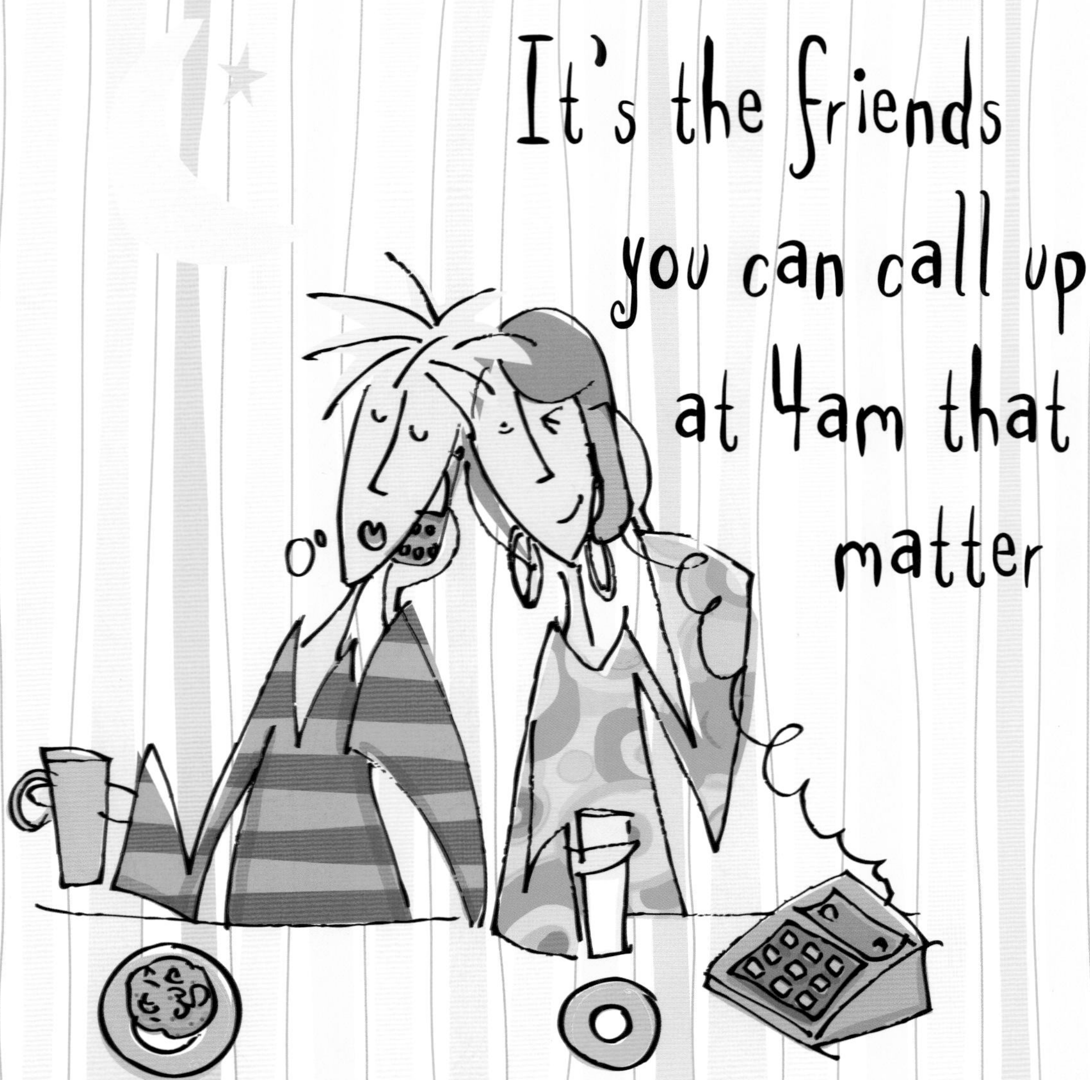
It's the friends you can call up at 4am that matter

A hug is
a great gift,
one size
fits all

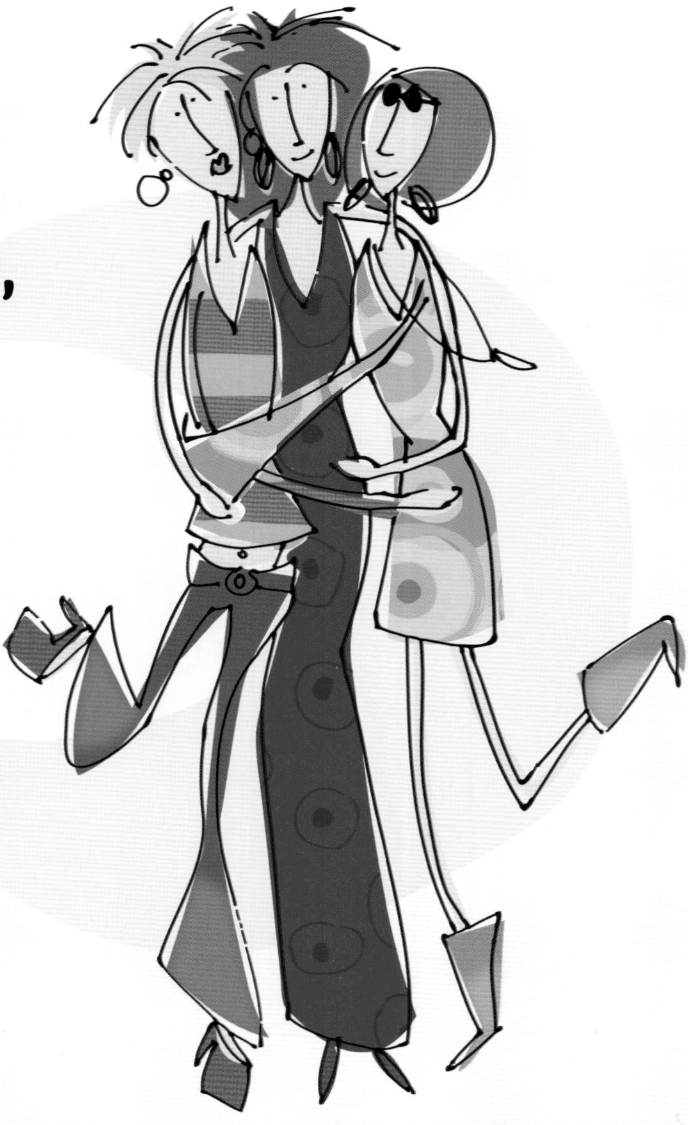

Friends welcome...
relatives by appointment

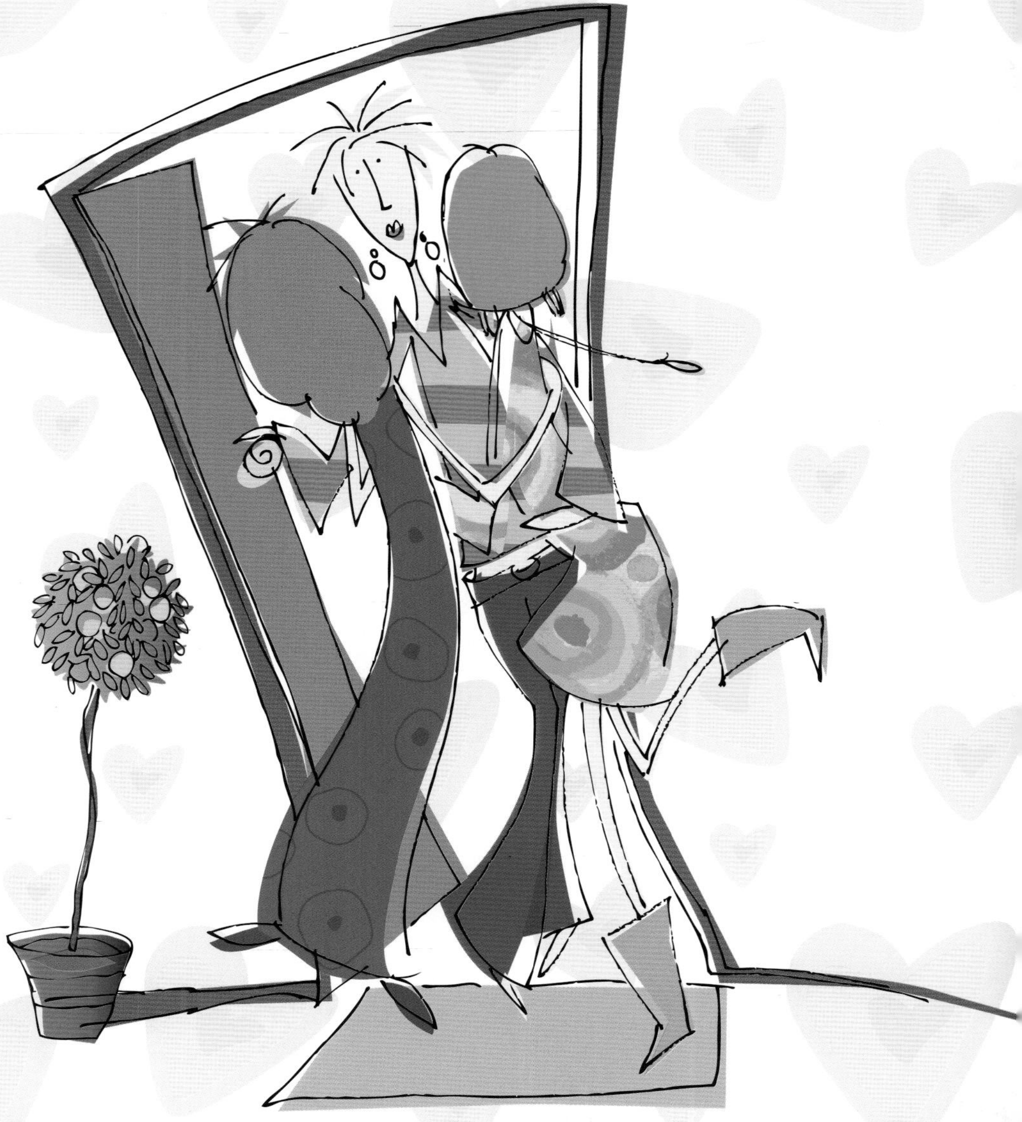

Friends are like flowers, they brighten your day

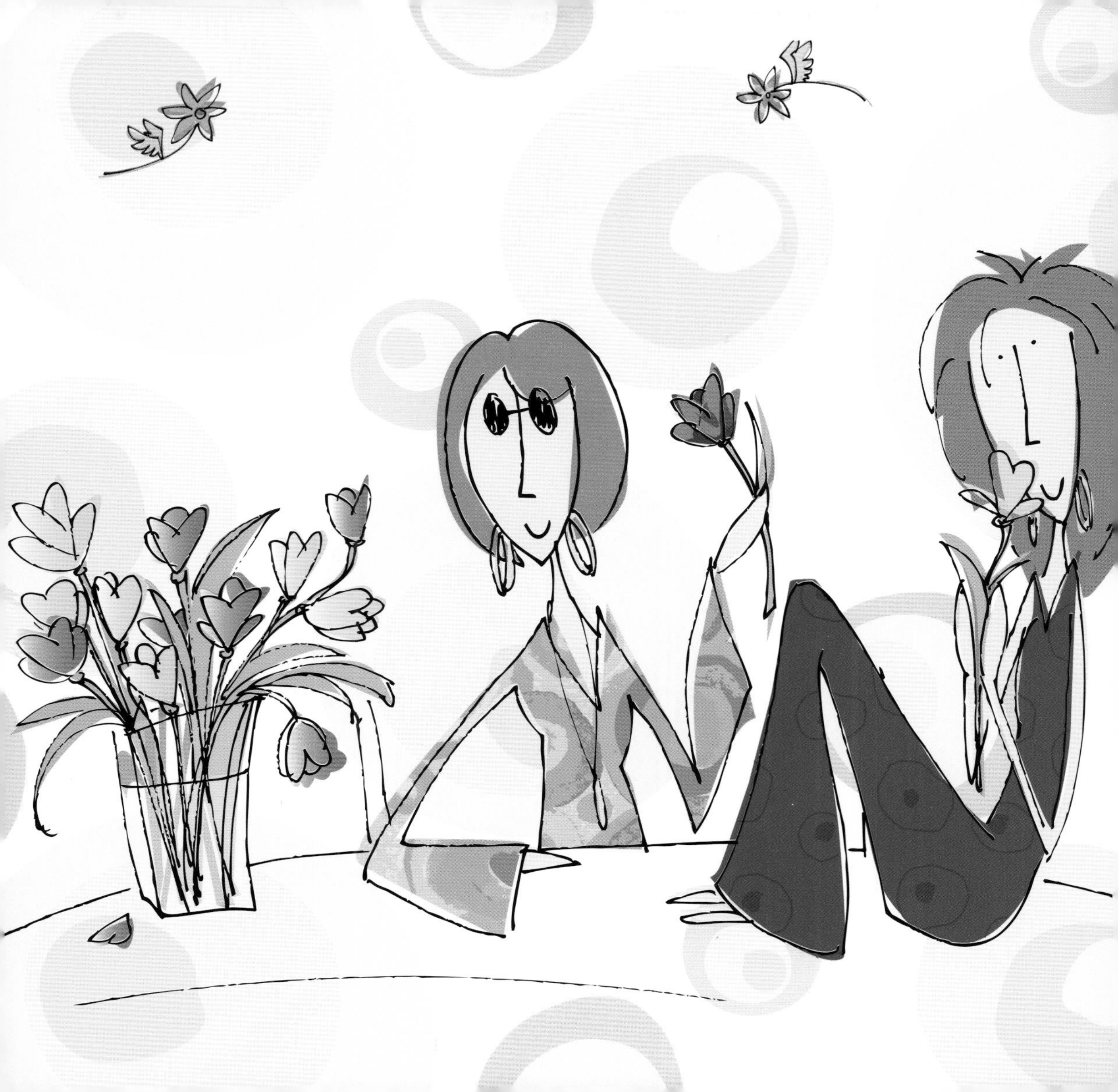

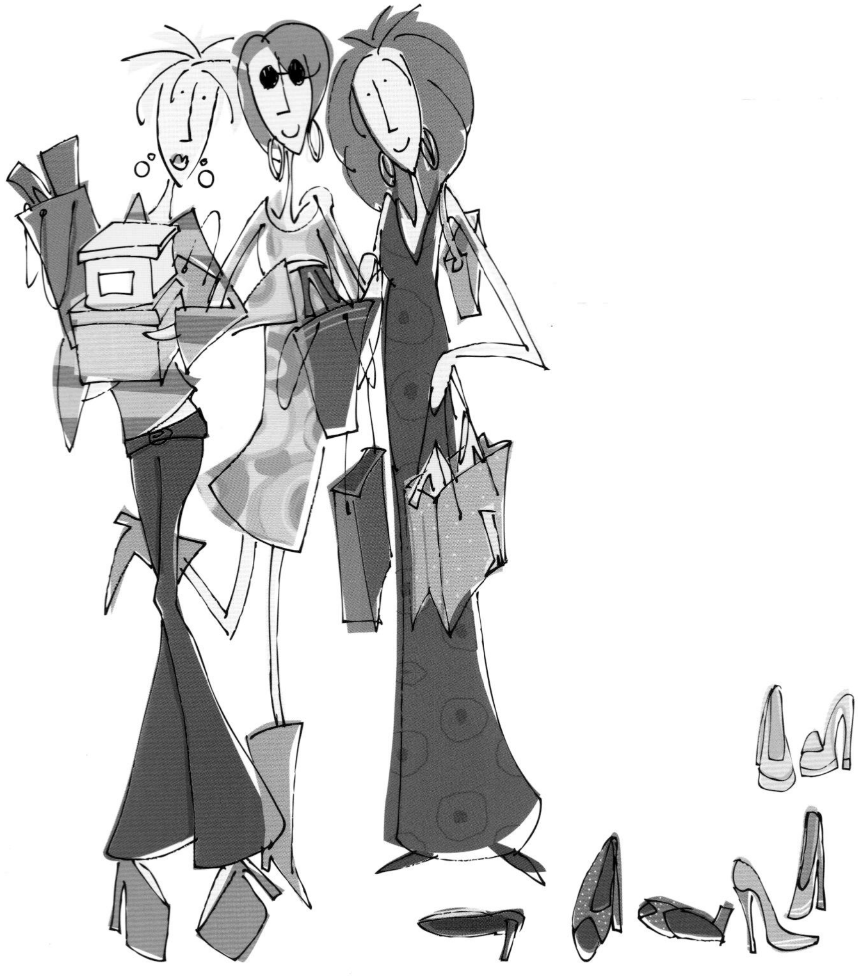

Born to Shop

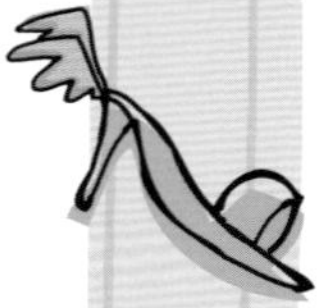

The years have been kind, it's the high heels that have done the damage

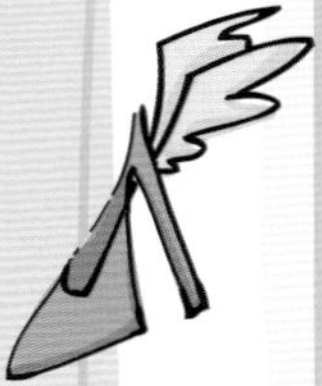

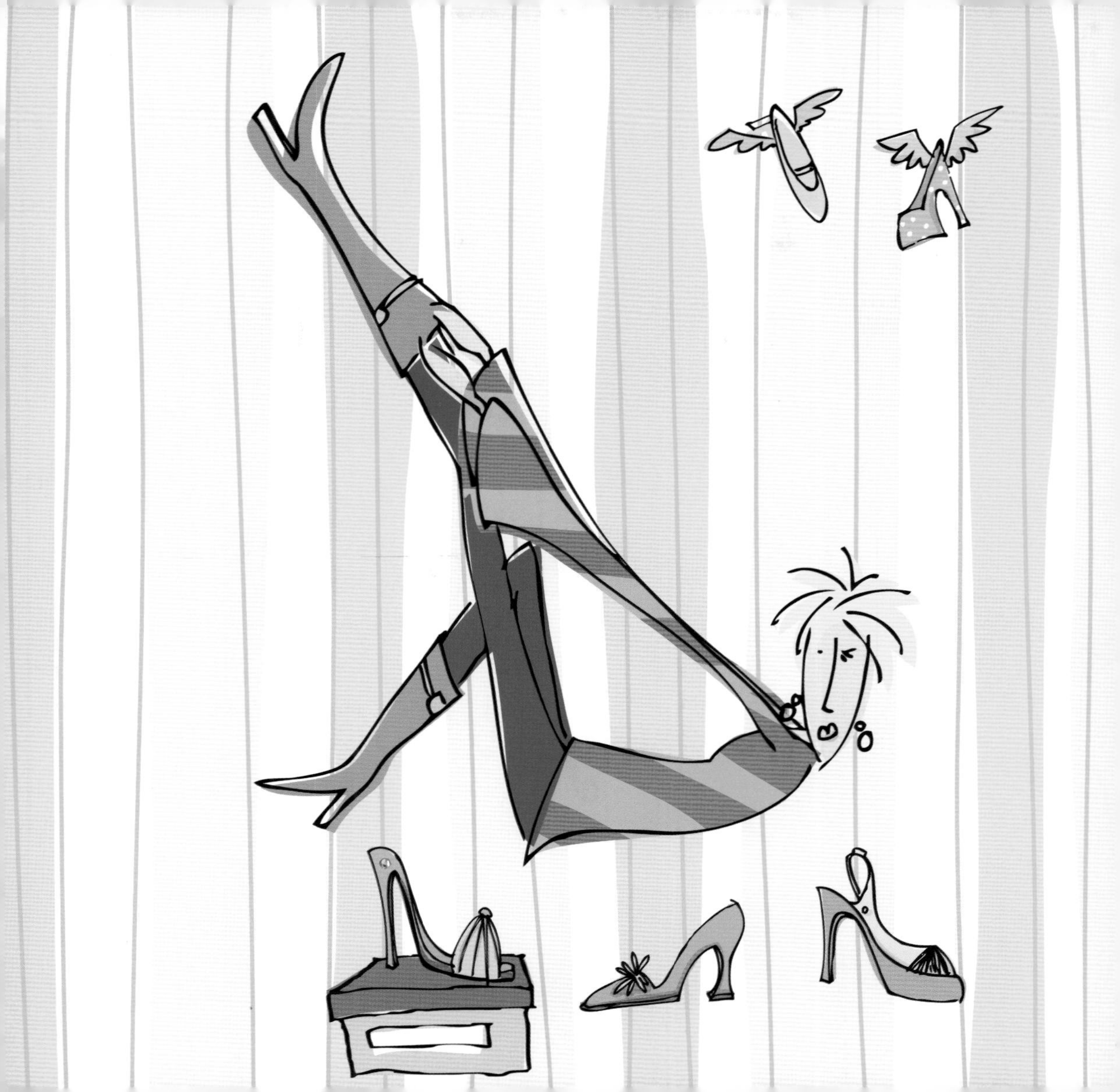

I've shopped all
my life and still have

nothing to wear

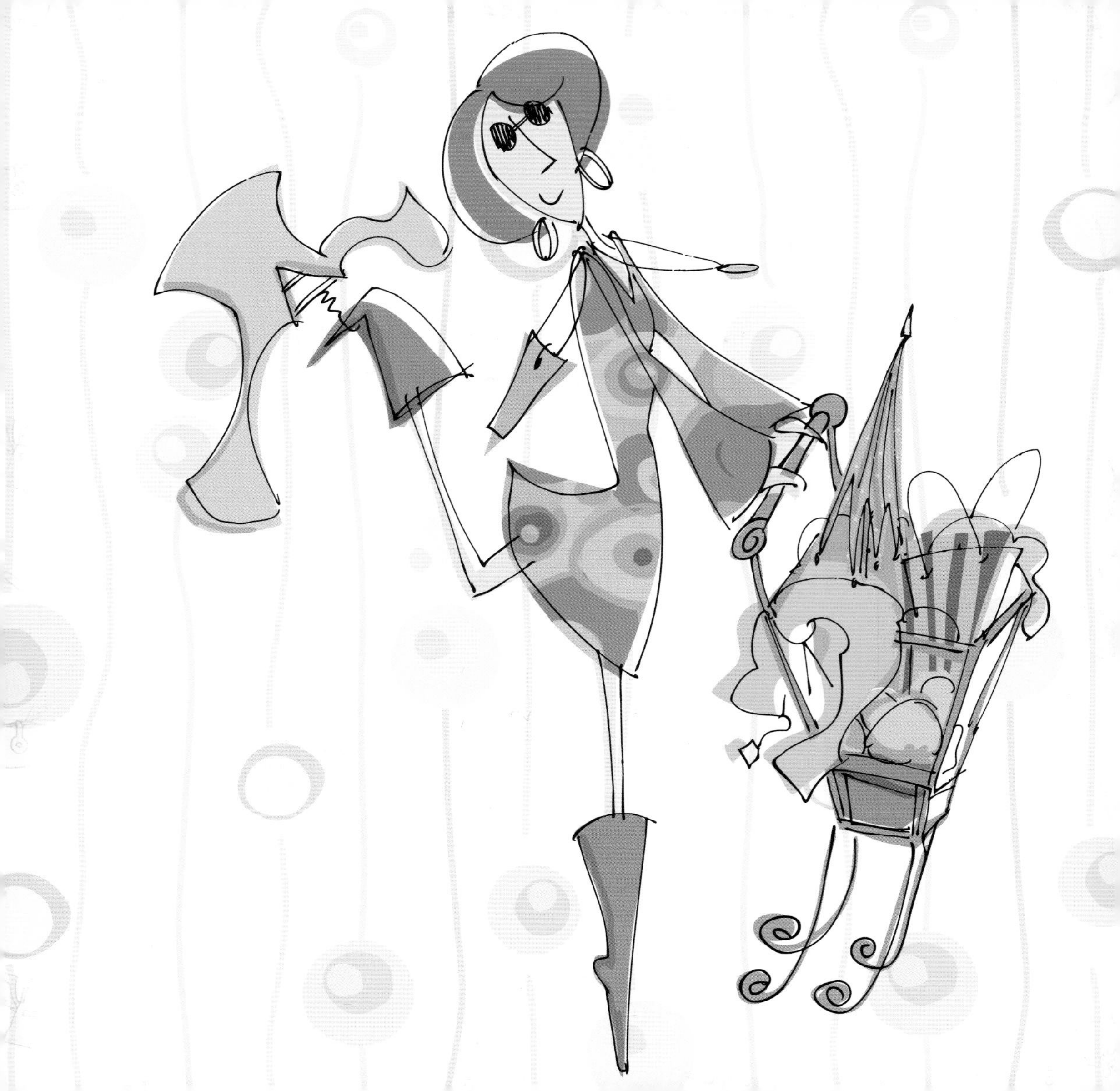

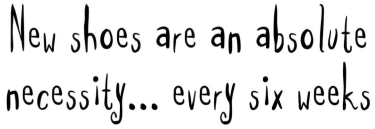

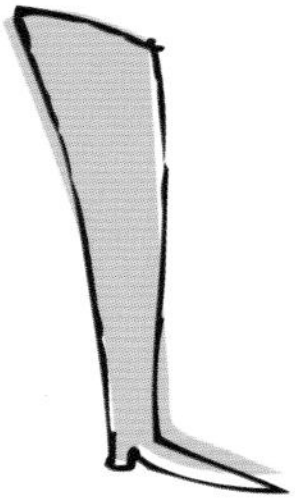

New shoes are an absolute
necessity... every six weeks

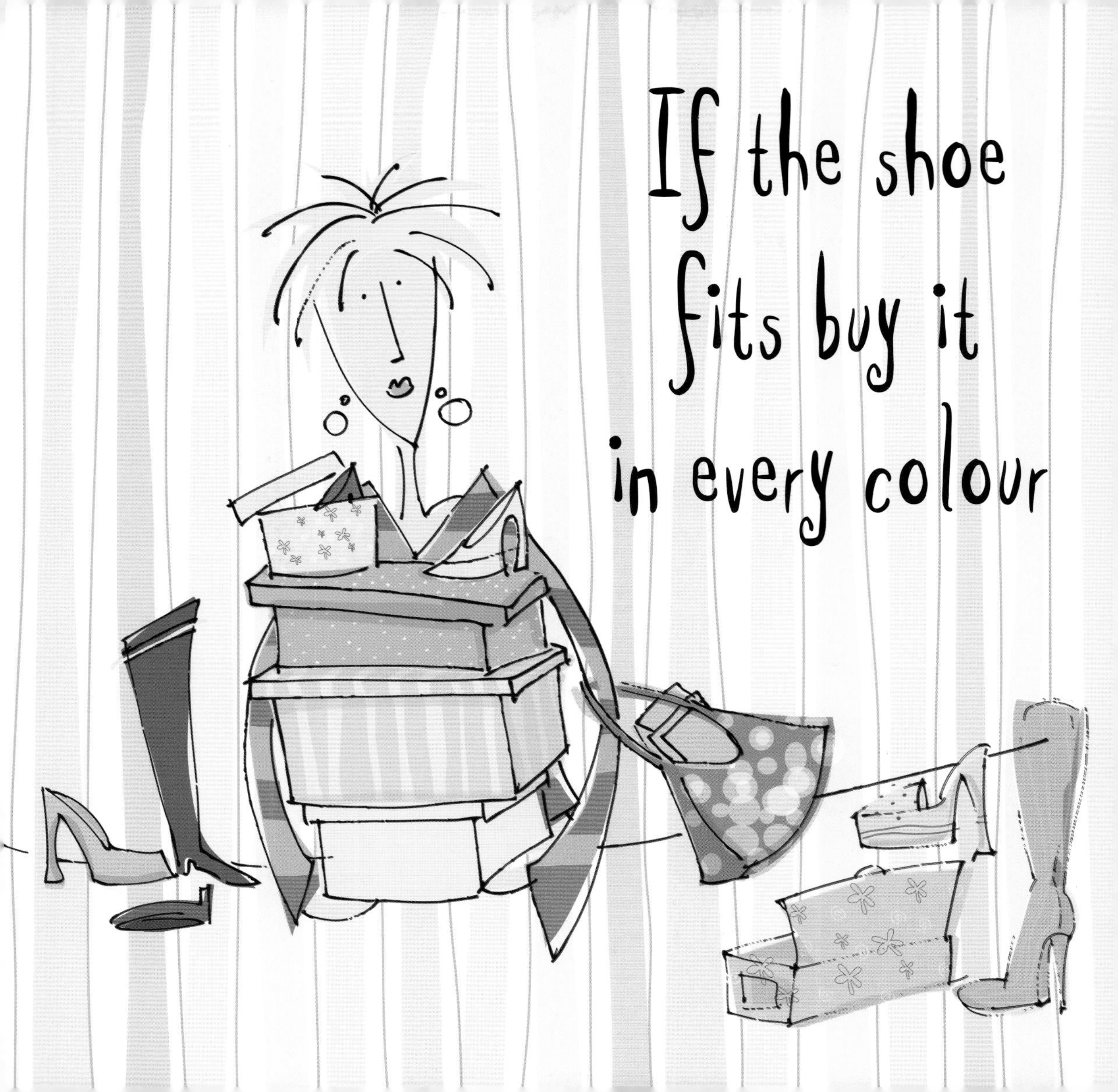
If the shoe fits buy it in every colour

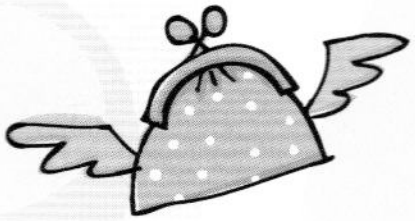

Let me shop and nobody gets hurt

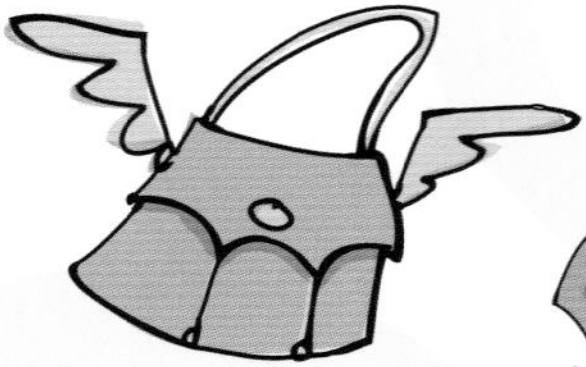

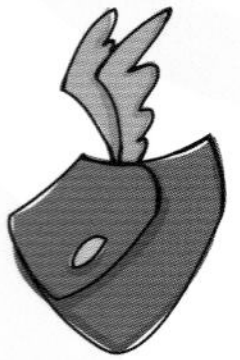

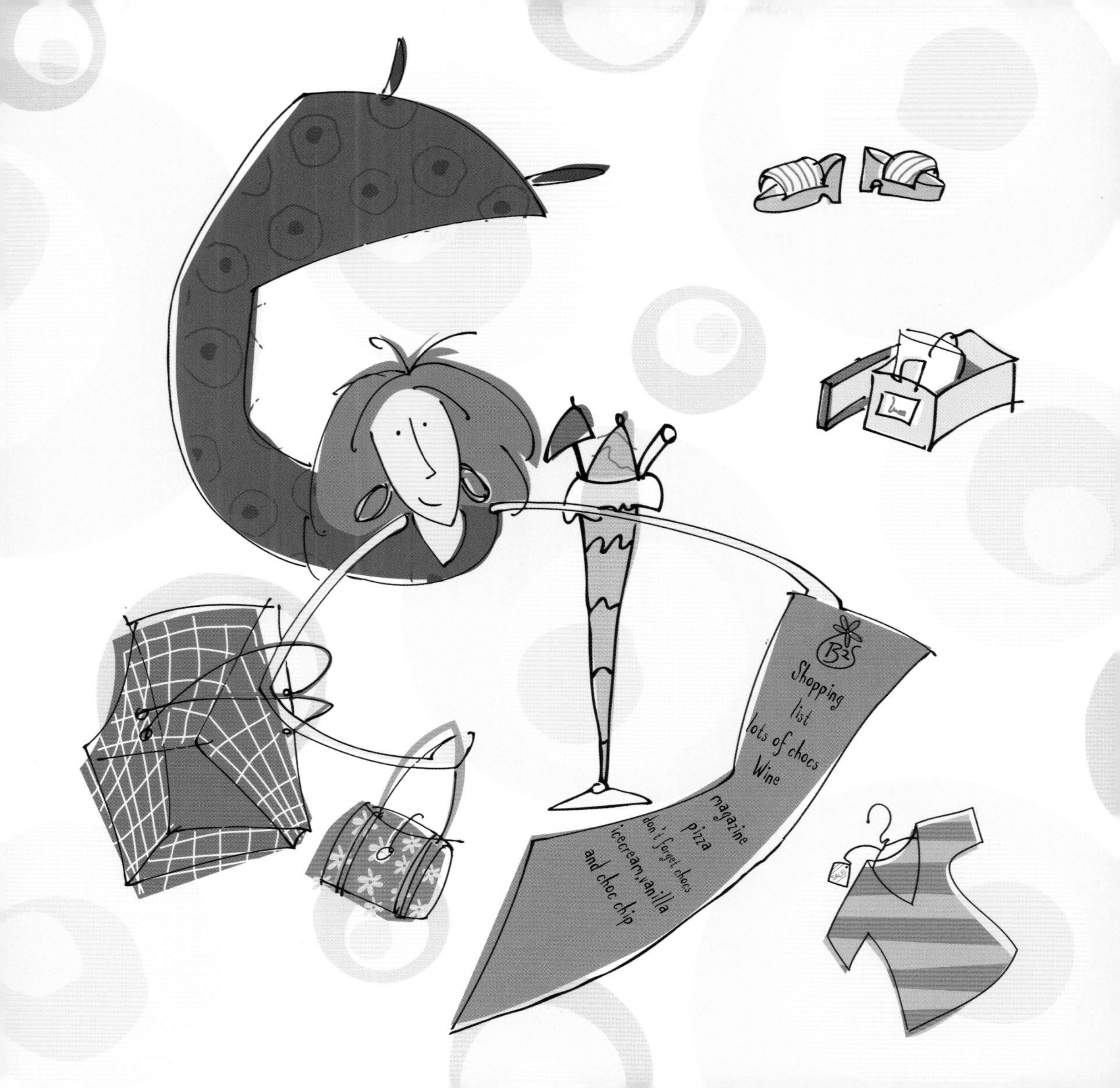

Shopping
list
lots of chocs
Wine
magazine
pizza
don't forget chocs
icecream, vanilla
and choc chip
SALE

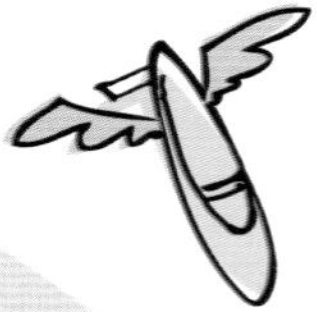

I need therapy...
retail therapy

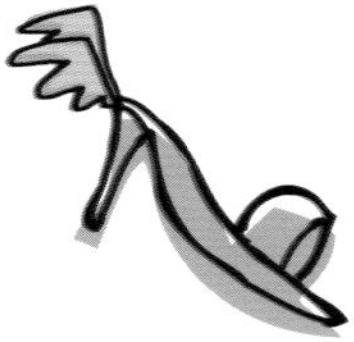

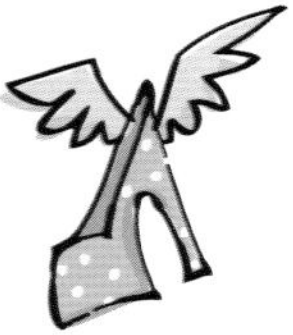

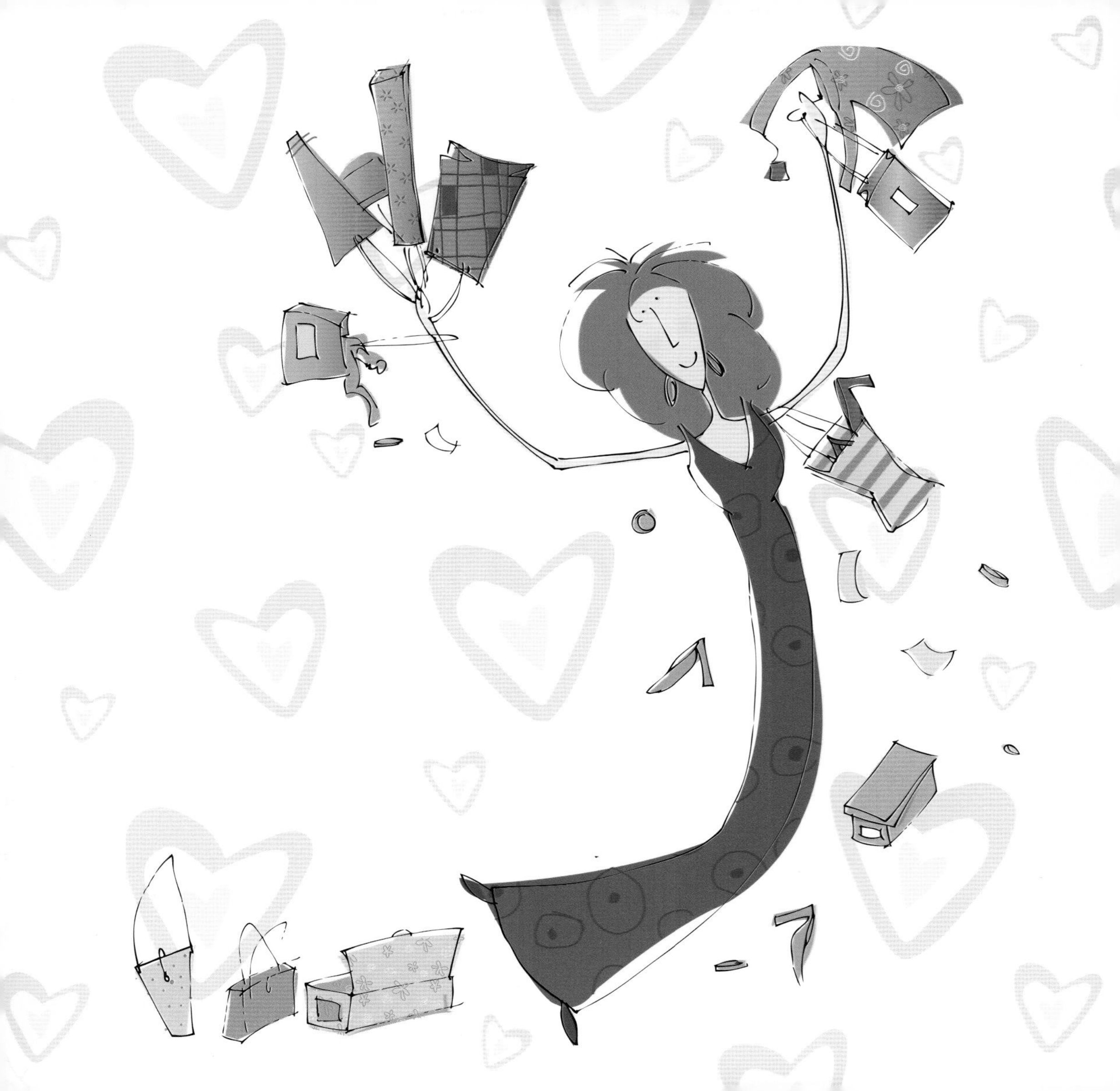

I'm having an
out-of-money
experience

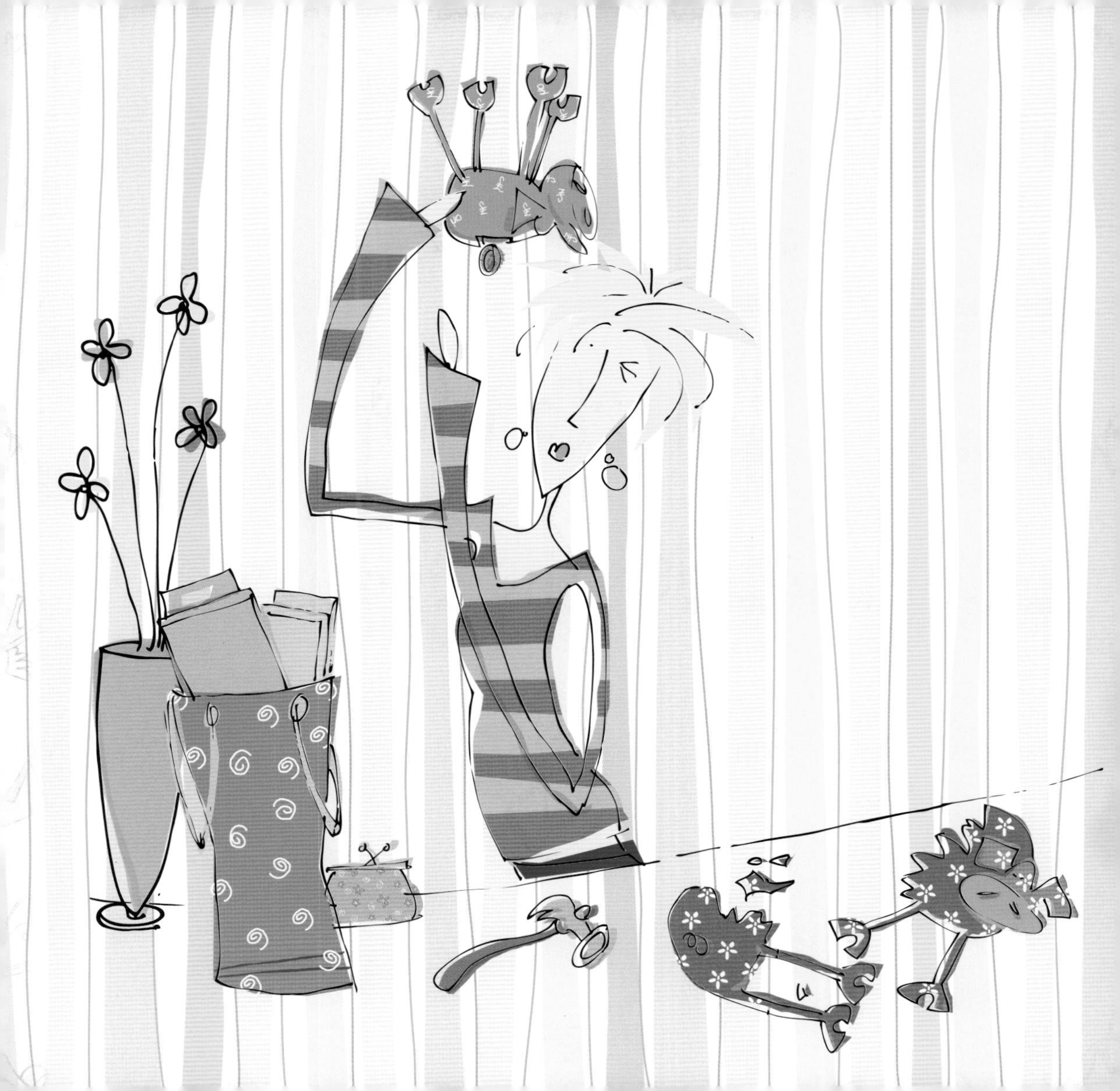

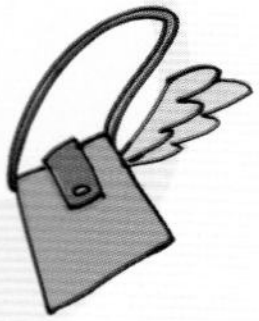

Born to Shop whatever the weather

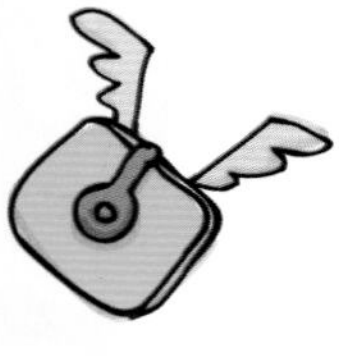

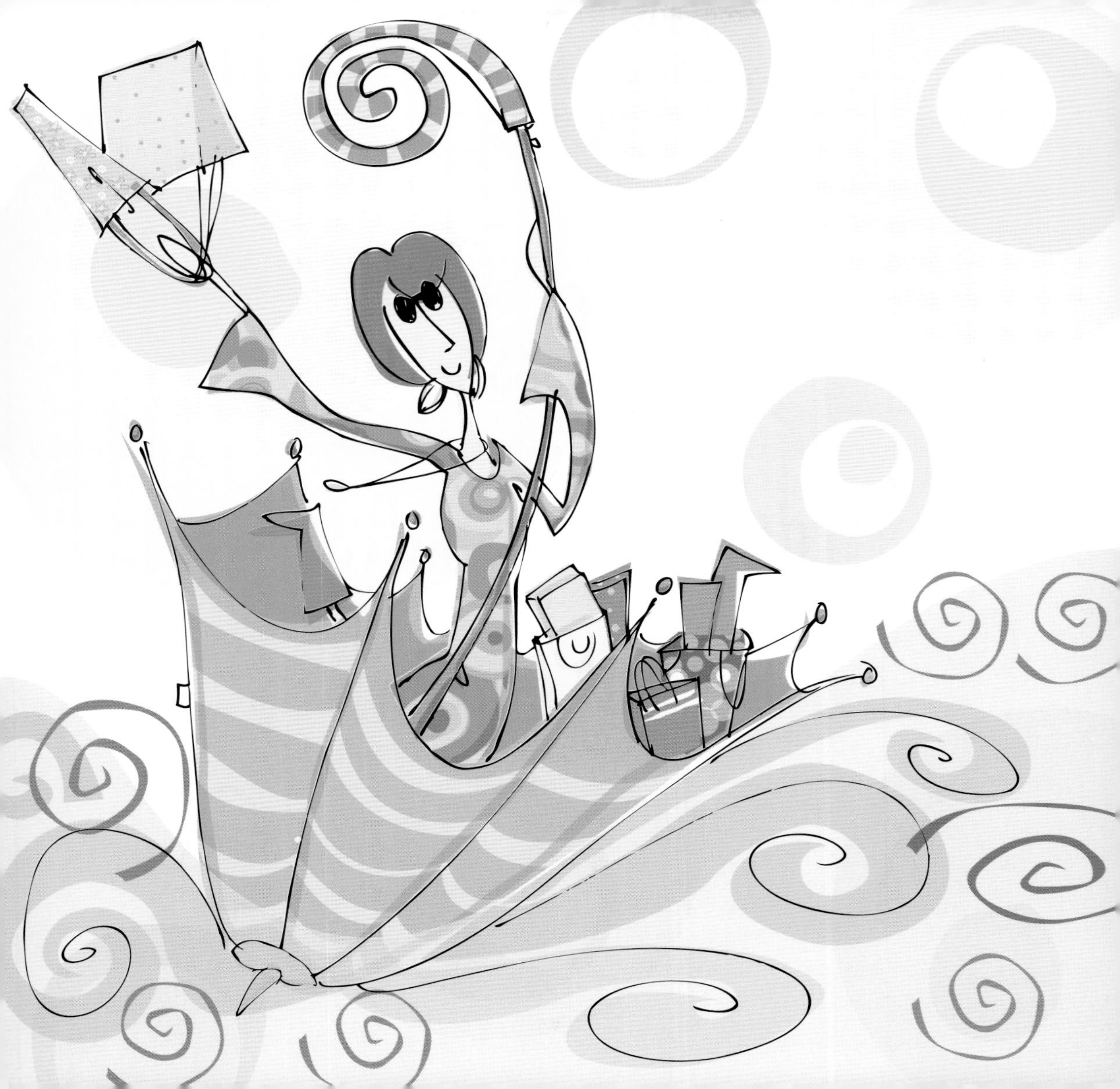

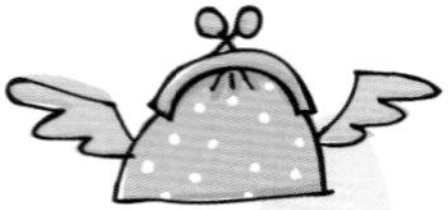
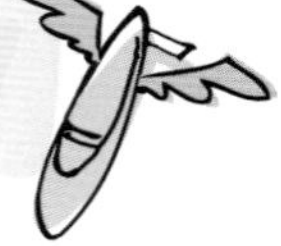

If at first you
don't succeed...
...buy buy again!

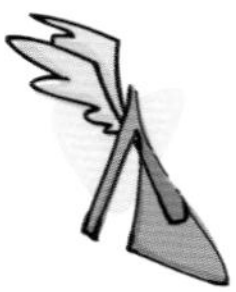
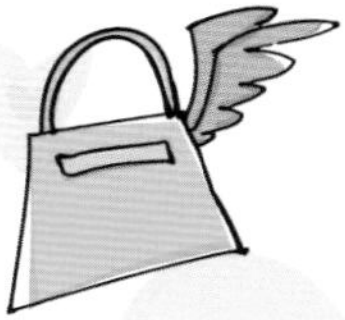

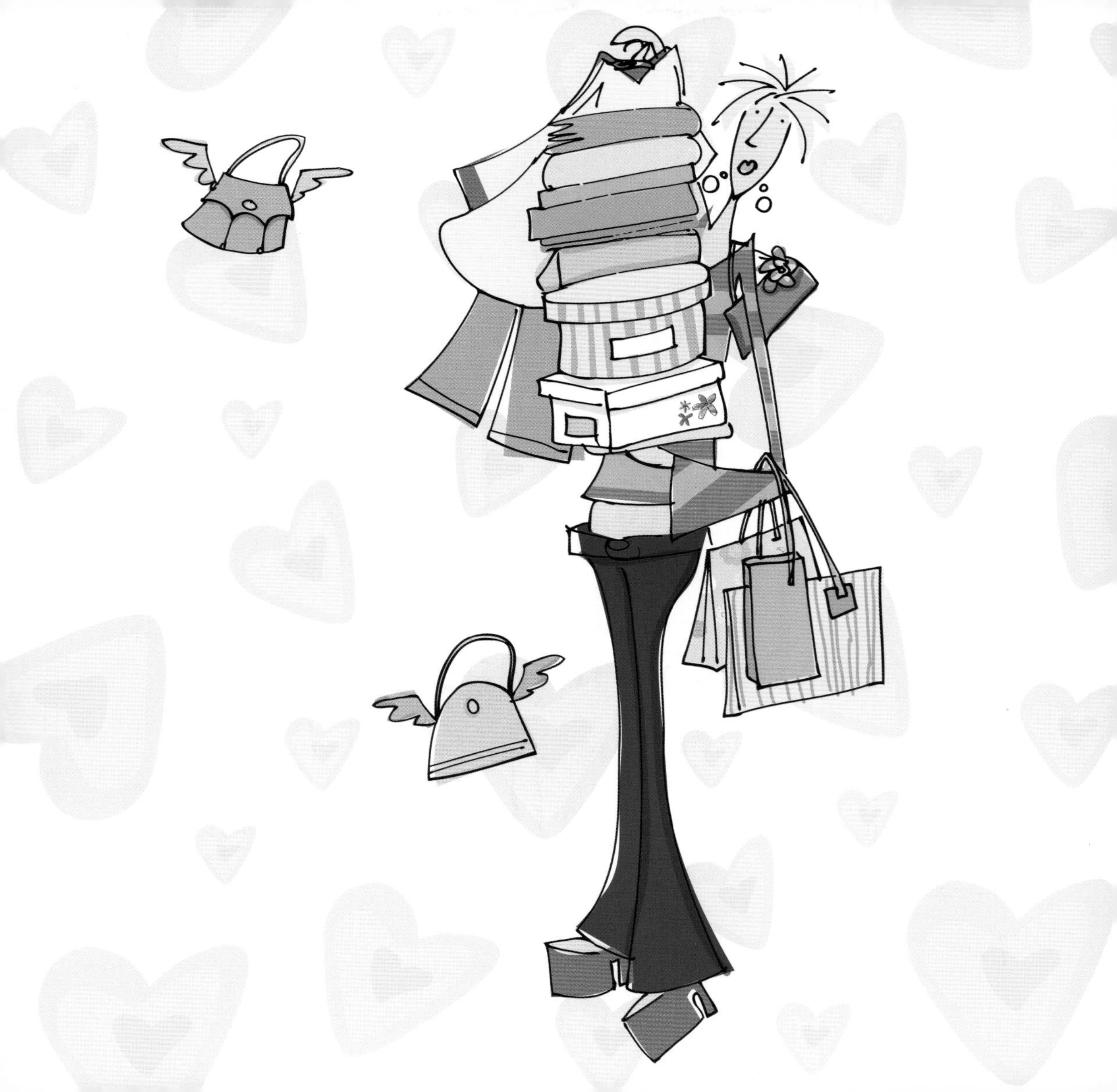

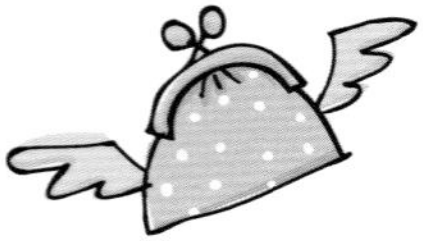
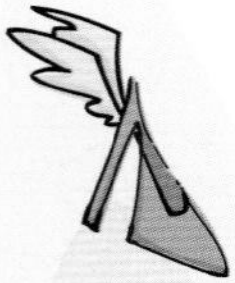
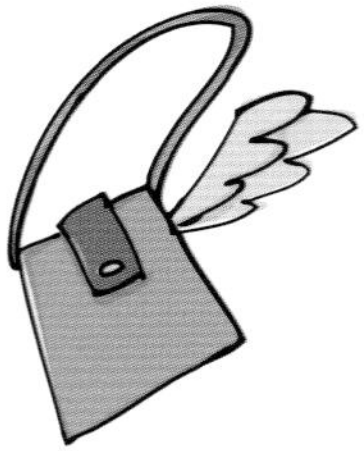

I enjoy the little things in life... shoes, handbags, jewellery

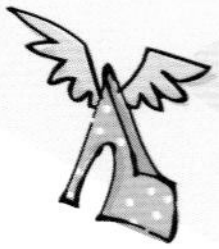
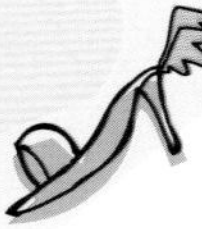
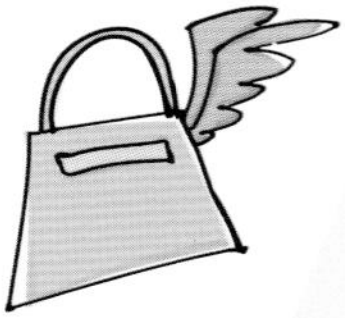
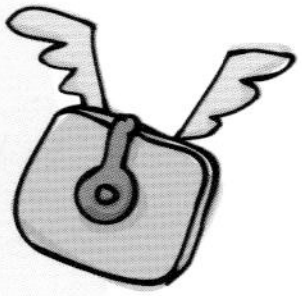

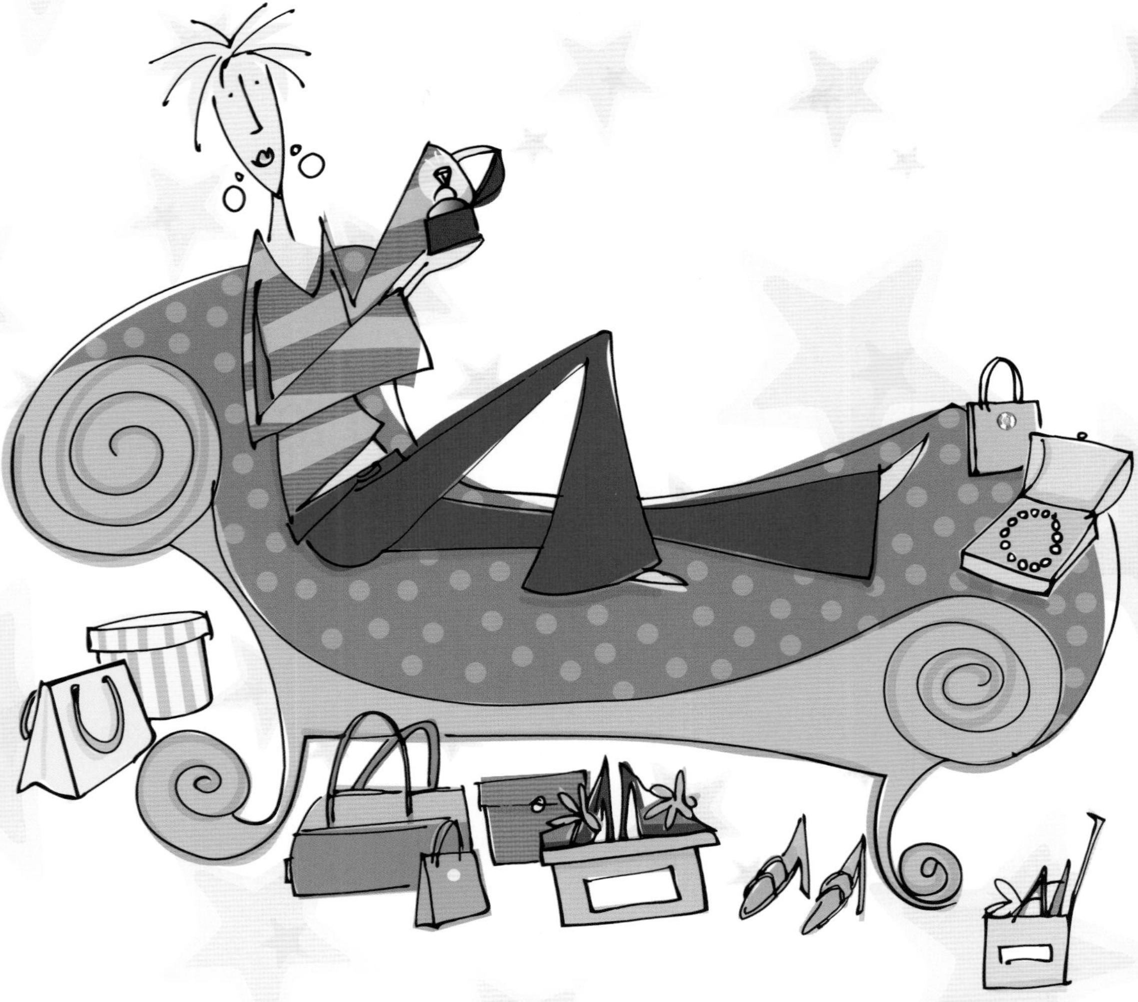

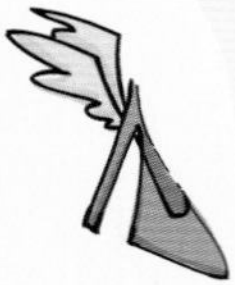

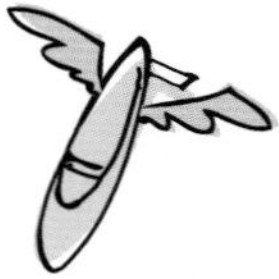

I can resist anything – except temptation

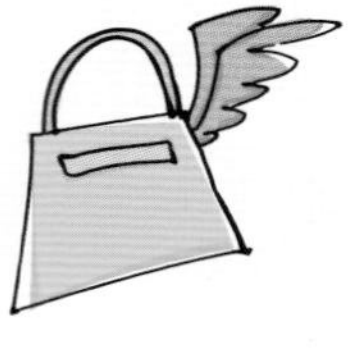

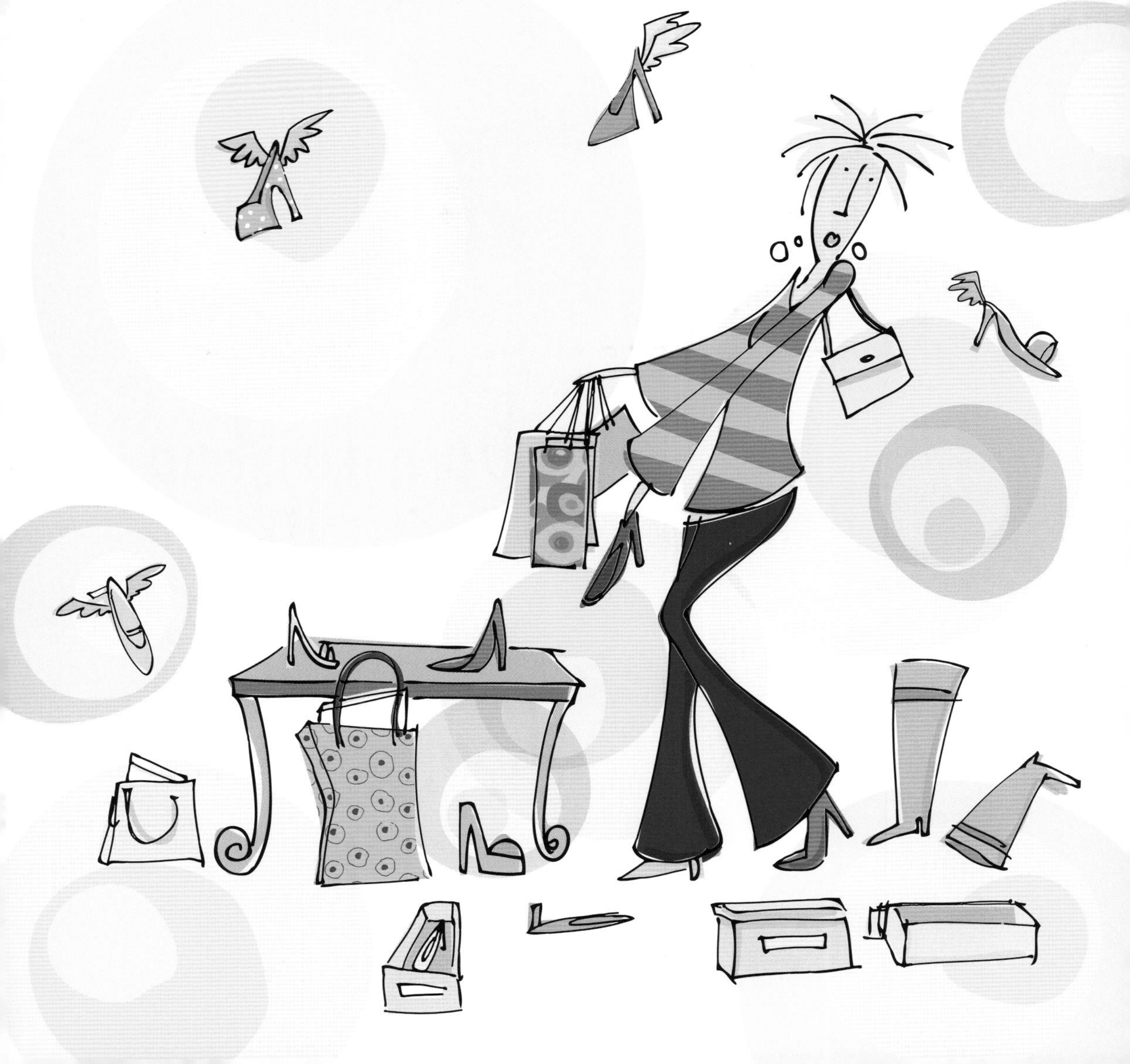

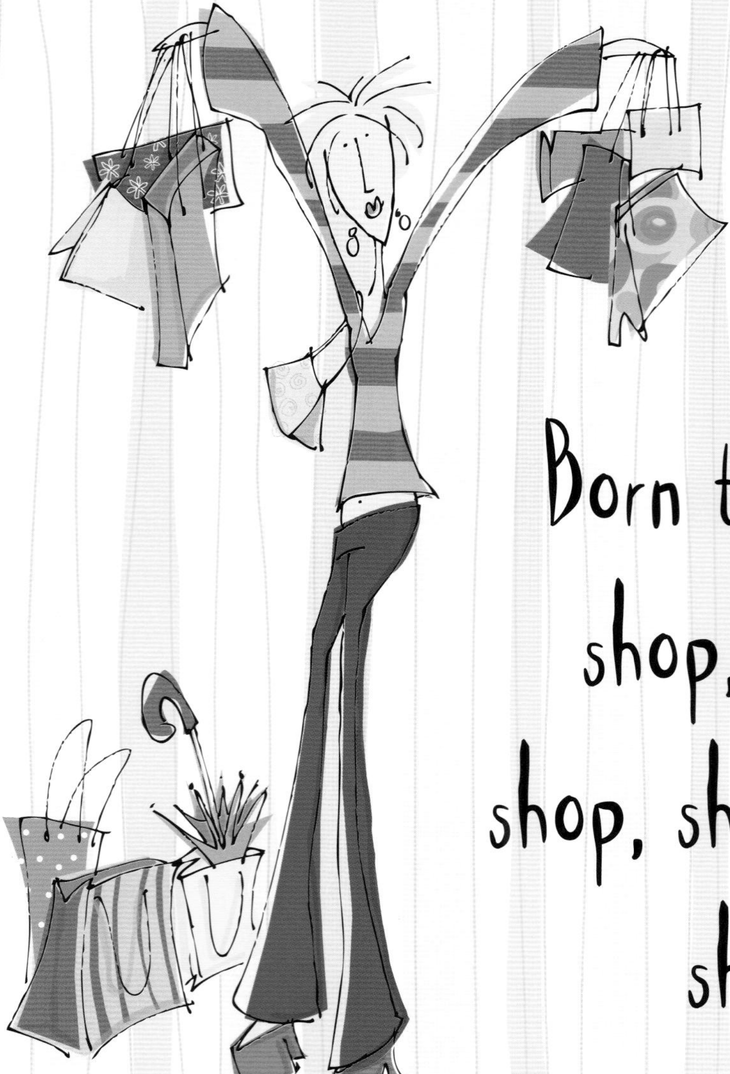

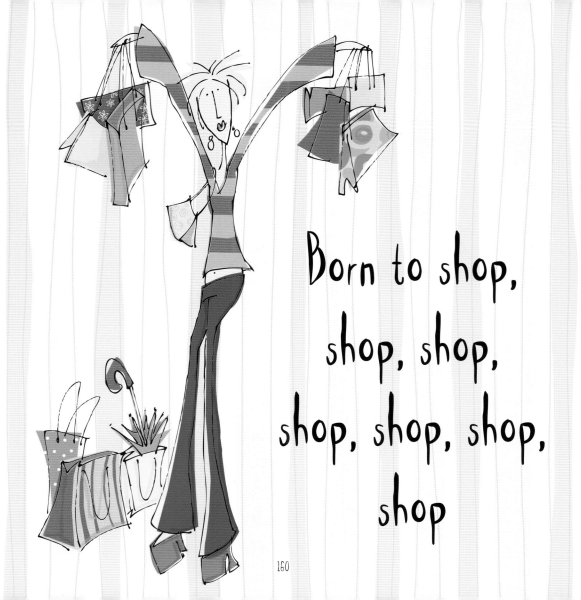

Born to shop,
shop, shop,
shop, shop, shop,
shop

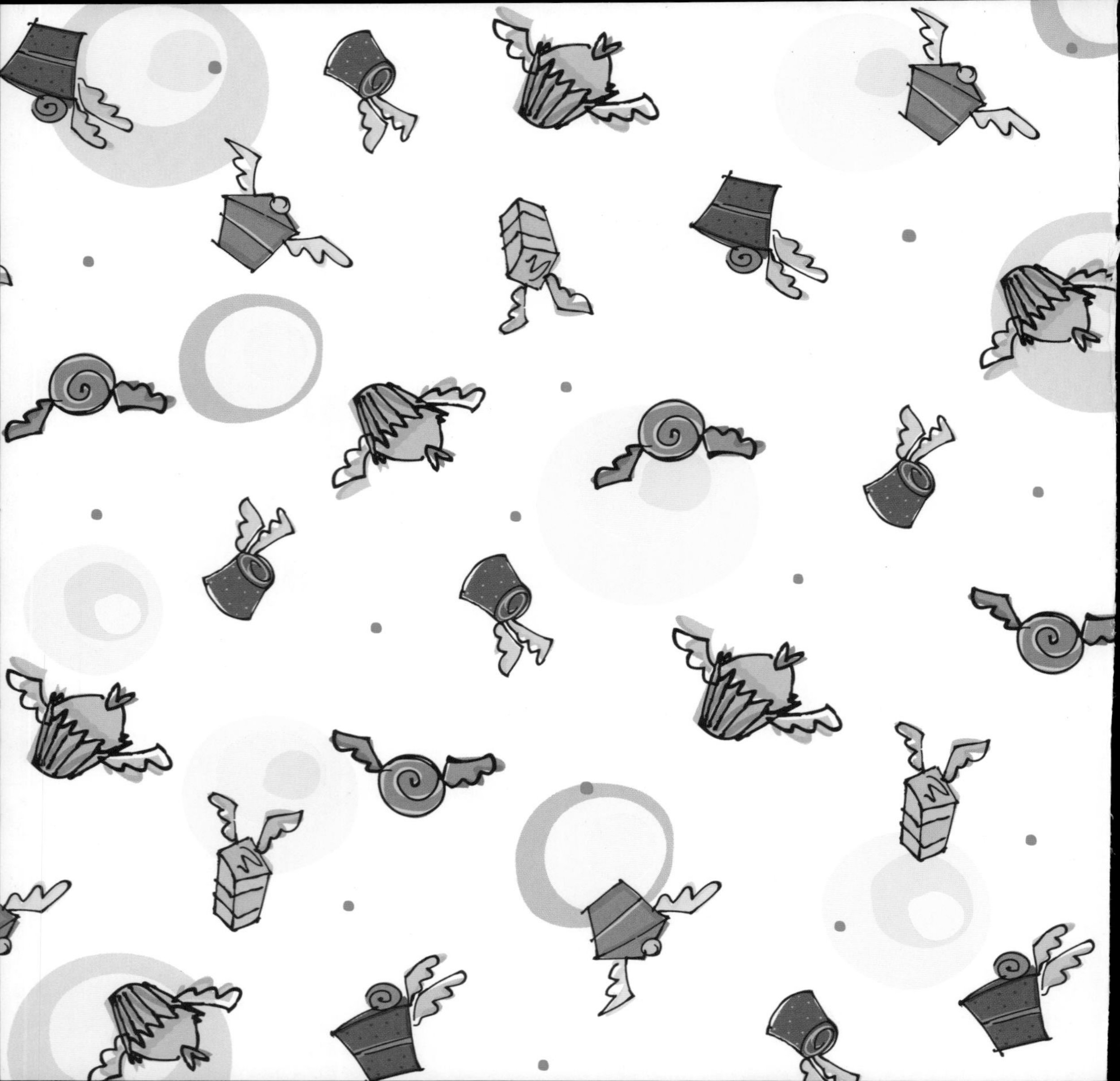